Today, workplace wellness and health promotion is seen by many as a wise investment in human capital. For the enlightened executive, improved employee mental, emotional and physical health is seen as an effective means of achieving a sustainable competitive edge. For the enlightened individual, seizing the opportunity that this book offers is one pathway to a healthy, fulfilling life.

Praise for *Bring Your Work to Life*

In *Bring Your Work to Life*, author Bill Mills addresses important life questions, and better still, assists us through great exercises to answer these questions in our own life. Don't just read this book, use it to do just what the title says!

— Tanis Helliwell, author of *Take Your Soul to Work*

Making our lives and our work meaningful is the greatest, most important—and most difficult—challenge any of us will ever face. Fortunately, Bill Mills gives us a shed full of remarkable tools that will help us cultivate that meaning and reap the joyous fruit of a fulfilled life!

— Ian Percy, author of *The 7 Secrets to a Life of Meaning*

Bill Mills offers a hands-on guide to help reveal and focus our path in bringing 'all of ourselves' to what we do. *Bring Your Work to Life* is a must for all of us who believe that performing at our best and achieving compassionate and meaningful communities in our workplaces are integrated parts of the same whole.

— Dan Stepchuk, Senior Manager, Organizational
Development, Corel Corporation

The balance of emotion, poetry, and imagery with rational analysis and planning in *Bring Your Work to Life* is powerful. Bill Mills' examples are believable, engaging, and illustrate his points very well. This is an important contribution to enjoying work and life.

—Jim Clemmer, author of *Firing on All Cylinders*

In today's world of uncertainty and constant change, it is easy for individuals to become confused and lose sight of their gifts and competencies. This book provides valuable exercises and examples that enable people to really determine their strengths and to align them with their organizations.

Bill Mills' focus, in terms of assessing the attributes of Self, of Others, and Higher Values, is a valid one. It is only when these three systems are aligned that we can truly expect greater commitment to the needs of the organization and the wider community.

— Margaret Butteriss, Independent Consultant
and former SVP of Fidelity Investments,
author of *Help Wanted: The Complete Guide to
Human Resources for Canadian Entrepreneurs*

Bring Your Work to Life is also about bringing life to your work. It has you look deeply, authentically and creatively at who you are, and more importantly, who you want to be, at work. If you want your work to be more meaningful, fun and of service to yourself and others, GET this book.

— Martin Rutte, co-author of *Chicken Soup for the Soul® at Work*

Bring Your Work to Life

Applying the Best of You to What You Do!

CREATIVE BOUND INC.

Resources for personal growth and enhanced performance
www.creativebound.com

Published by Creative Bound Inc.
Box 424, Carp, ON
Canada K0A 1L0
(613) 831-3641   info@creativebound.com

ISBN 0-921165-78-1
Printed and bound in Canada

Production by Baird O'Keefe Publishing Inc.,
Publication Specialists (613) 831-7628
    Gail Baird, Managing Editor
    Wendy O'Keefe, Creative Director
    Janet Shorten, Text Editor

Author photograph by the *Ottawa Citizen*
Cover images © PhotoDisc

Printing number 10 9 8 7 6 5 4 3 2 1

National Library of Canada Cataloguing in Publication Data

Mills, William John, 1951-
  Bring Your Work to Life : applying the best of you to what you do! /
William J. Mills

ISBN 0-921165-78-1

1. Job satisfaction. 2. Self-realization. I. Title.

HF5549.5.J63M54 2002   650.1'3   C2002-903884-7

It is with sincere gratitude and warm
affection that I dedicate this book to

Donald E. Smith, Ed.D.,

who has been my friend, mentor and
colleague for the past twenty-seven years.

Acknowledgments

I would like to acknowledge the following people for their inspiration
and generous contribution to the creation of this book:

**My clients and the many people
who have participated in my workshops**
Thank you for challenging and inspiring me.

Gail Baird
who guided me skillfully through the publishing process

Janet Shorten
who made this book more readable

Wendy O'Keefe
who designed an amazing final product

The many friends who attended my pre-publication book party
Your enthusiasm was contagious and inspiring.
The wine, beer and scotch helped a lot, too!

**My parents, Edward and Leona Mills,
and my in-laws, Harry and Joyce Samson,**
who have given me their unconditional love.

My son
Ben
who has shown me the virtue of
patience and the power of play

My son
Adam
who constantly models how to build
authentic relationships with ease and grace

My wife and colleague
Margaret
who offered encouragement, support
and insight throughout the writing process
You have always been my first and final point of reference.

Contents

Bring Your Work to Life:
Applying the Best of You to What You Do!

Work is the sandbox of life. It's where grown-ups go to play. How much of your time do you spend in the sandbox? Consider just your waking moments, for example. When you remove sleep from the equation, you will probably conclude that you spend more of your time at work than at any other activity. Most people spend at least half of their waking moments at work.

> Charlie Jacobson is the operations manager for the polymer cable product line at Polytec Wire and Cable Company. He has 17 years of work experience and this morning as he looks at himself shaving in the bathroom mirror, he reflects upon his work and his life.

> "Look at me," he thinks. "I've been doing this for 17 years. I get up every day at 6:00 a.m., shower, shave and head out to work, where I spend eight hours each day sitting in meetings, writing reports and keeping the line running. Then I come home, have dinner, go to bed, and then get up and start all over again. Some life!"

How much meaning do you derive from your work, since this is where you spend half of your time? Unfortunately, many people experience work as a series of dispirited interactions undertaken solely to further the cause of the organization. Moreover, the organization's purpose might be only vaguely related to the personal needs and aspirations of the individual employee. Consequently, work becomes "meaningless."

Meaning is a powerful motivator. It leads to both personal and organizational commitment and success. For Charlie and many others, however, the experience of work is devoid of real meaning, and motivation becomes a continual and frustrating challenge. This is true for a surprising number of organizations and individuals.

You go through the motions. You find that on Monday you look forward to Wednesday, "hump day." You know that if you can hang in there, you'll be able to climb the hump and then slide down the hill to Friday. On Wednesday, you tell yourself Thursday is the unofficial start to the weekend—and after all, Friday is TGIF.

Come Saturday, you're on your own time—or are you? The weekend represents, for most of us, the time of the week you look forward to, the time of the week when you are the master of your own fate, when you can do what you want when you want to. Or can you? Our personal time is so full of necessities and obligations, it's often hard to find time just for ourselves.

Think about this weekend, for example. What are your plans? What's on your TO DO list? Do any of these items look familiar?
- Do the grocery shopping.
- Take the kids to soccer, baseball, gymnastics, music lessons…
- Drive your son or daughter to a friend's house for a sleepover.
- Pick up Grandma for a visit.
- Go to the bank.
- Get a haircut.
- Cut the lawn/water the grass/shovel the snow.
- Phone your sister.
- Do the laundry.
- Take the car in for servicing.
- Fix the leaking tap.
- Buy light bulbs.

- Make dinner for friends on Saturday night.
- Go out to a movie.
- Attend a volunteer function.
- Help a friend move.
- Weed the garden.

So it's hard to find time just for ourselves—even on the weekend. But if we could, what would that mean for our overall work–life balance? Work five days a week so you can spend two days a week doing what you'd really like to do? Work 49 or 50 weeks a year so you can spend two or three weeks a year doing what you'd really rather be doing? Work 25 or more years so you can spend the balance of your life doing what you'd truly like to do?

What's wrong with this picture? Are you truly deriving enough meaning and motivation from your work? Is your work–life out of balance? Would you change it if you could? Of course you would.

The truth is, you can. That's what this book is about. It will show you how to bring your work to life. It's all about connections, and it goes further than the familiar phrase, "It's not what you know; it's who you know." Your level of work satisfaction is really determined by how you connect. "It's not who you know; it's how you connect." This book will show you how to get more meaning out of your experience of work, so you're not wishing this precious time away. Time is life. If you waste your time, you waste your life.

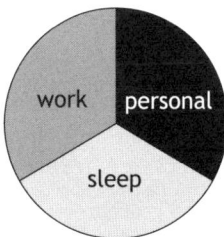

How we spend our time in life

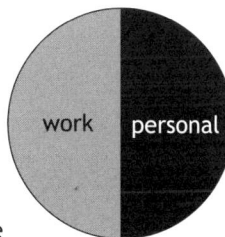

How we spend our waking moments

Did you ever see the movie *Groundhog Day*? In it, a television weather reporter, played by Bill Murray, finds himself in a seemingly endless repetition of the same day—Groundhog Day. He wakes up at 6:00 a.m. and goes through the events of the day, only to find that when he wakes up the following morning, it's the same day as the day before. Everything becomes predictable. All the events he encounters, the people he meets—all of his interactions—are the same as the day before. He's caught in a hamster wheel, living out an endless repetition of the same Groundhog Day, over and over again.

That is, until he learns to connect. Through the movie, he gradually manages to transform his life by developing a genuine relationship with, first of all himself, then with the other characters he meets during the day, and finally, with a sense of higher purpose and values.

In short, he takes a dispirited existence and transforms it into a meaningful life.

To activate meaning and motivation in your work and your life, you need to understand the importance of relationships. Relationships are to life what the atom is to matter. They are the fundamental building blocks of existence. Relationships are not just important—they are all that matters. The secret to activating meaning as a motivator in your work is the exploration and development of three key relationships:

- Your Relationship with Self—connecting with who you are and what you want;
- Your Relationship with Others—connecting with people as individuals and as teams;
- Your Relationship with the Higher Values—connecting with life's universal principles.

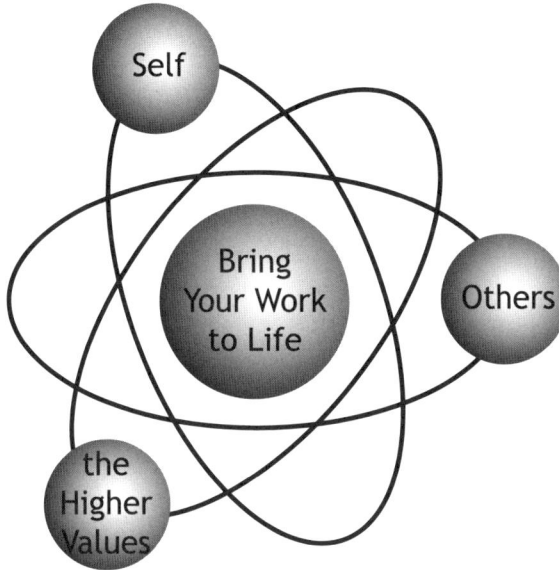

• • •

Relationships are to life what the atom is to matter.
They are the fundamental building blocks of existence.
Relationships are not just important—they are all that matters.

• • •

This book is filled with a multitude of practical models, anecdotes and exercises. They will show you how to connect with and develop each of these three essential relationships.

The first part of the book deals with your relationship with Self. This consists of knowing who you are and what you want, understanding how you invest your time, taking your personal values into your workplace, achieving a reasonable work–life balance, taking care of your personal resources of body, mind and spirit, and bringing your consciousness to everyday events.

The second part of the book explores your relationship with Others. This centers on treating others with compassion, communicating with sensitivity and honesty, and making a conscious effort to transform your work group from a loose collection of individuals into a genuine community.

Finally, the third part of the book treats your relationship with the Higher Values. This involves defining your personal operating philosophy, identifying which Higher Values are most relevant for you right now, and ultimately, transforming ideas into action.

Life is short—and almost half your waking time is spent at work. So seize the opportunity that this book offers. Instill more meaning and motivation into your own work. Bring your work to life. Apply the best of you to what you do. Get up Monday morning saying to yourself, "Thank God it's Monday; I get to go to work again today!"

Part One

Your Relationship with Self

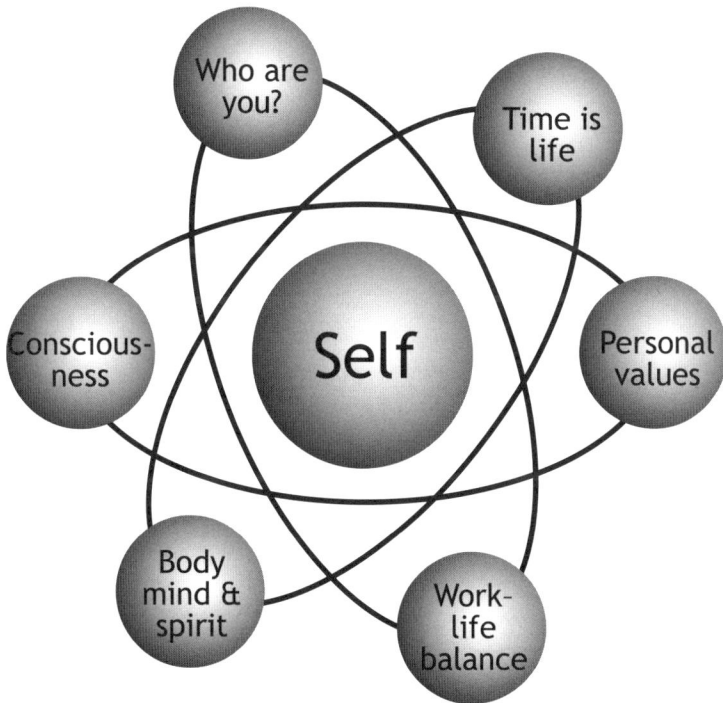

Y ou are walking along a beautiful downtown street on a sweet summer's night. There's music and a hint of perfume wafting through the air. You're passing in front of a nightclub. The music is irresistible. You can tell it's a live band. People are laughing and dancing on the sidewalk. You approach the solid brass doors and notice the marquee. The band's name is LIFE. Part of you would like to check it out; part of you is a little afraid because you are all alone. What should you do? You decide to approach the large, shiny doors and ring the bell. Suddenly, a small panel in the middle of one of the doors opens up. A face appears. "Who are you and what do you want?" he shouts above the music.

What would you say? Do you have a good answer to these two questions? How badly do you want to experience LIFE?

Very few people have thought about even the questions, let alone the answers. Yet they are at the very heart of who you are. Your answers help you define and understand your unique self. They help draw boundaries around you, distinguishing you from the other people in your life, thus making meaningful relationships possible. Relationships exist where our boundaries overlap. In order to connect with others, you first need to know where your own boundaries are.

> Riaz Mohanderson is a bright, young software engineer who works for a large telecommunications firm. In the 12 years since his graduation, he has worked for three different companies.

> He's friendly and competent. A lot of organizations would be happy to have him—and everyone seems to enjoy working with him. He feels good knowing that he could get a job almost anywhere.

This morning, out of the blue, an employment agency phones him. There's a very good position available with another high-tech firm in Toronto, and the starting salary is excellent.

He fumbles through the unexpected telephone interview trying to sound interested and yet not really knowing if he actually is. There seems to be good rapport between himself and the recruiter. The recruiter wants to take things to the next level. He is inviting Riaz to Toronto for a more serious, follow-up interview.

Should he go? Should he turn it down?

It feels really good to be wanted, to be in demand. But he's making good progress where he is, too. What would his wife and children think about the possibility of moving to Toronto, a full day's drive from their hometown?

What would be good for his career? For his family? What is important to him? Is this just a work decision or is it a life decision? What does he really want?

In truth, he doesn't know.

Finding meaning and motivation in your work depends a great deal upon how clear you are about who you are and what you want. Your relationship with Self is the first of the three fundamental building blocks of life, and your answers to these questions are essential. There are no shortcuts. In the following pages are a few exercises designed to help you gain more clarity about your answers.

The first exercise, called *My Top Ten*, presents 10 questions that focus on the results you'd like to achieve in life, the contributions you would like to make, and the kinds of personal qualities you would like to emulate. The following two exercises will assist you in determining *Who am I and what do I want?* and in creating a clear and concise Statement of Purpose.

Answer all the questions spontaneously. Your first answers are probably your best. Move through the questions quickly and creatively. Have fun along the way and make sure to record your answers.

Have you ever seen children playing with building blocks? Typically, before they begin to play, they spread the blocks all over the floor, take several moments to mentally take them all in, and only then begin to play. Your answers to these exercises are like that. They are the building blocks from which you will begin to create your vision of who you are and why you are here.

Excercise 1: My Top Ten

The Things I Would Like to Have

What are some of the things I would like to have? Keep in mind that "haves" might be tangible possessions (e.g., a mansion on a lake) or they might be intangible (e.g., a happy family).

_____

_____

_____

_____

_____

_____

_____

_____

_____

The Contributions I Would Like to Make

If I were a billionaire, how would I occupy my time?

_____

_____

_____

_____

When I look at my work life, what do I consider to be my greatest strengths and accomplishments?

_____

_____

_____

_____

What activities and interests most absorbed me as a child?

_____

_____

_____

_____

What do I consider to be my most important future contribution to others?

_____

_____

_____

_____

What talents and interests do I have, whether developed or undeveloped?

_____

_____

_____

_____

The Qualities I Would Like to Emulate

Who has served as a valuable role model for me and has had a significant and positive impact in my life?

_____

_____

_____

_____

What qualities does this person possess that I would like to emulate?

_____

_____

_____

_____

In Summary...

I would like to be someone who...

_____

_____

_____

_____

Five years from now, I would like to have realized the following goals:

_____

_____

_____

_____

Excercise 2:   Who Am I and What Do I Want?

This second exercise serves as a bottom line. It will give you a tangible idea of where your boundaries are, what comprises your unique self, and in short, who you are and what you want.

This exercise consists of a continuous writing experience, and as such has very specific guidelines. When done effectively, it can reveal information to you that you would not have been able to access otherwise.

The technique of continuous writing is analogous to brainstorming with other people, except in this case you are brainstorming with different areas of your own consciousness. This experience can only be achieved to the extent that you are able to adhere to the following guidelines:

At the top of a piece of paper, record a question that you would like to address. For the purposes of this exercise, your question should be consistent with "Who am I and what do I want?"

- Other versions of this question might include such possibilities as: "What is my purpose?" "Why am I here?" "What is most important to me?" "What is it that I would like my life to be about?" It is essential that you choose a question that is meaningful to you.

- Once you have chosen your question, answer it by writing for 10 minutes without stopping.

- When you can't think of anything else to write, write exactly that. The idea is to write exactly what you are thinking.

- No judgment. No editing. As in brainstorming, accept any idea, any spelling, any grammar, any *thing*!

Exercise 3: My Statement of Purpose

Review what you've just written in the continuous writing exercise. Underline the ideas that are of highest value to you.

Based on these ideas, write between one and three sentences in the box below that best represent the answer to your question. This is your Statement of Purpose—a statement that reflects who you are and what you want.

_____

_____

_____

_____

_____

_____

_____

_____

_____

_____

_____

_____

_____

Sample Statement of Purpose

Here is an example from a previous workshop participant.
Note that a Statement of Purpose is unique to the individual who wrote it.
Therefore, yours needn't resemble this one at all.

Be all I can be.

Do all I can do.

Respect all.

Remember life is short.

So, always have fun!

Riaz was caught off guard by the call from the employment agency—sometimes life is like that. In the meantime, though, he has sounded out his wife and children about the possibility of relocation. He has also had a chance to reflect upon who he truly is and what he wants out of his work-life. He has reaffirmed his sense of purpose and has re-committed himself to providing a stable environment for his children while they're still in school.

Although decisions of this nature are rarely easy, at least Riaz is now clear about what he wants to do. His decision? He would love the job in Toronto and his wife would love to relocate—but not now. That kind of move will have to wait a few more years until the children have finished high school.

How about you? You're offered a promotion. Another company wants you. Your boss asks you to volunteer for a special task force. A colleague needs you to help out on a project. Should you accept? Should you turn it down? What would be the impact on your current commitments? On your family? On your friends? On your Self? It feels really good to be wanted, to be in demand. But what is important to you? Is this just a work decision or is it a life decision? Who are you and what do you want? It's good to know.

Your relationship with Self is the first of the three fundamental building blocks of life, and being clear about your own purpose is essential.

The next chapter focuses on how you spend your time. Time is an investment and a limited, non-renewable resource. The next chapter will help you examine where you've been, where you are and where you're going, so that you can end up with the work and life that are consistent with who you are and what you want.

Time Is Life

Time is life. How you choose to spend your time is how you choose to spend your life. Your investment of time is an outward reflection of your relationship with Self. Some people protect their investments. Others are very haphazard about how they use precious resources such as time.

This chapter looks at where you've been, where you are right now and where you're going, so you can end up with the work and life that fulfill you.

Since time is a resource, let's compare it with another familiar and precious resource, namely money. Do you have enough money? Most people would probably laugh and say "no." Now, how about time? Do you have enough time? Again, most people would probably laugh and say "no." And yet, this is really not logical.

Think about money, for example. What portion of the world's wealth do you have? Not much, most likely. So it is logical that you could want more. Compare this with time. How much of the world's time do you have? Of course, you have just as much time as anyone else. You might feel that you don't have enough time, but in reality—and unlike money—you already have all there is. The only question then is, how do you spend it?

In the previous chapter, you refined your notion of who you are and what you want. This chapter provides you with an opportunity to create the future that best reflects that notion. This is essential for establishing an effective relationship with Self.

There are several exercises that follow. They will assist you in creating a life history, including the lessons you've learned along the way and the kind of future you'd like to realize. You will also have a chance to analyze your current use of time and energy. Are you investing your time in matters that are truly important to you? Do you have enough personal energy to pursue your dreams? What would your work and personal life consist of, ideally?

Exercise 4: My Tree of Life

Reflect upon your life history. Divide it into eras of 10 years each, starting from as far back as you can remember, and extending it as far into the future as you would like.

Then, identify one or two key events that stand out for you (or that you would like to stand out for you) from each era.

Finally, choose a word, phrase or symbol to represent each era and record it in the tree in alignment with the corresponding number.

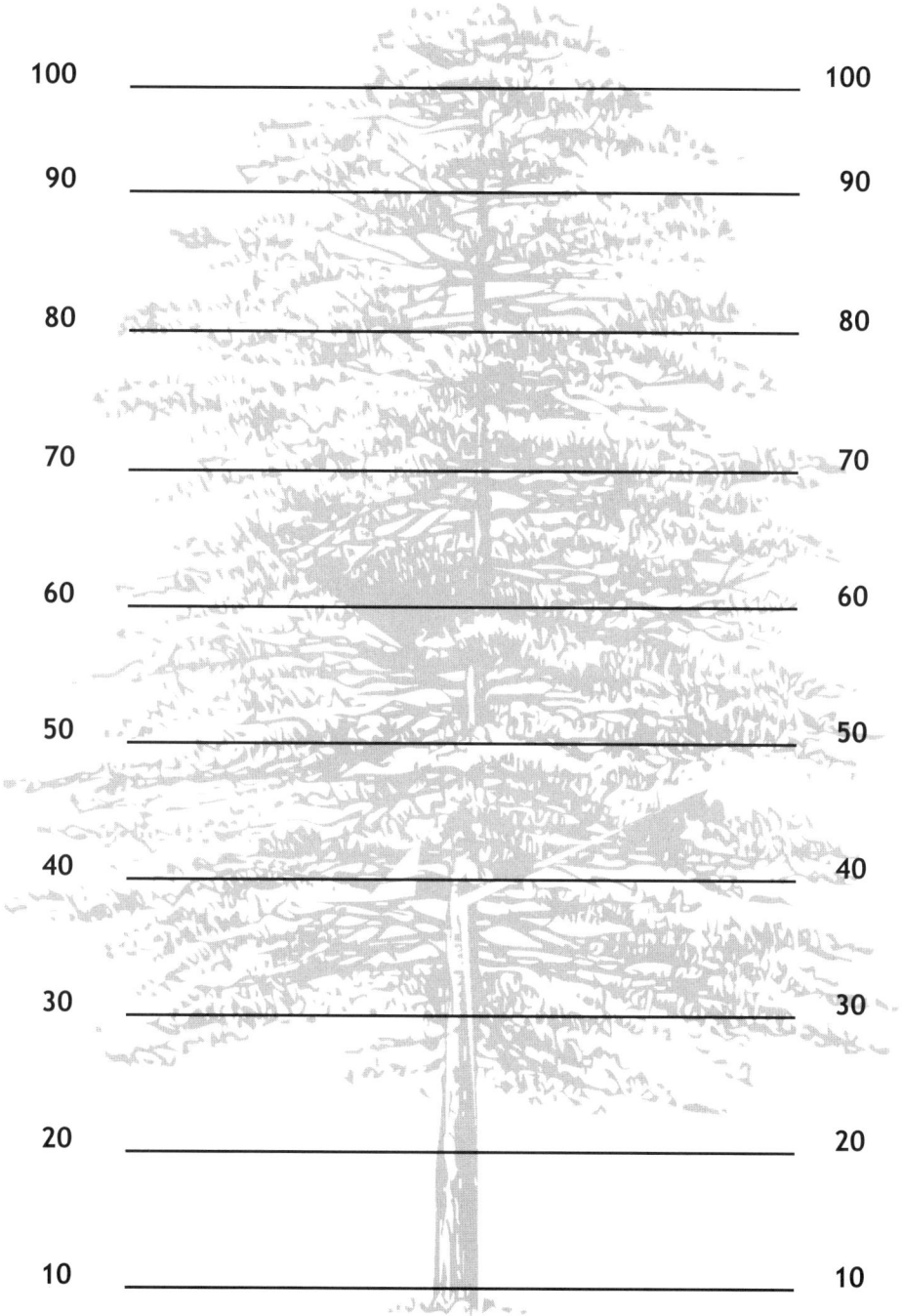

100	————————————————	100
90	————————————————	90
80	————————————————	80
70	————————————————	70
60	————————————————	60
50	————————————————	50
40	————————————————	40
30	————————————————	30
20	————————————————	20
10	————————————————	10

Once you've created your Tree of Life, review where you've been, where you are now, and where you're going. Then answer the questions below:

What have I learned along the way from previous life events?

_____

_____

_____

_____

What themes or patterns do I notice about the kind of future I would like to create?

_____

_____

_____

_____

What could be a next step for me in creating the future I would like to have?

_____

_____

_____

_____

Creating the future you would like to have can feel like an overwhelming challenge. Most people have very full lives already. You might already have a busy job, a spouse and children, aging parents, friends who would like to see you a little more often, siblings and other relatives whom you'd like to stay in touch with, et cetera. So where do the time and energy come from to create a more fulfilling future? Take Jennifer's example:

Jennifer is the single parent of three elementary-school-aged children. During the day, she works as a technologist for a high-tech company. The work is steady, but it doesn't pay that well. Three nights a week she works in a local bar, serving drinks. The tips are good. She enjoys the social interactions in the bar and she needs the money. That's why she maintains the two jobs.

The problem is, however, she doesn't really like either job very much. She'd really prefer to become a lawyer or a legal assistant. She's always been interested in law. But the question is, how can she do what she'd really rather be doing, given all of her responsibilities?

She feels stuck. She feels locked in and out of control. Her time is really not her own. And besides, after working at two jobs all week, and looking after three kids, who has energy for anything else? By Sunday, she's close to collapse.

Jennifer understands herself well enough to know what she'd rather be doing. She'd rather be working in the legal profession. Unfortunately, she's stuck because although she has the desire, given her circumstances she doesn't have the energy to pursue it.

Have you ever found yourself with the time to do something important but you simply didn't have enough energy to get it done? Have you ever had the energy to do something important, but you simply didn't have the time? To create a more meaningful future requires managing both time and energy. To manage one without the other is frustrating and counterproductive. This is part of Jennifer's predicament.

Jennifer feels burnt-out because she's spending too much of her week on the treadmill. She feels locked in. Her time and energy are consumed by too many activities that are absorbing too much of her energy. She has run out of gas.

She simply doesn't have the resources to pursue her career goal.

Have you ever run out of gas? It's not a good feeling to come sputtering to a halt on the road of life.

The Quality of Time Matrix in the next exercise is an excellent tool that can help Jennifer understand her situation a little better. It might help you understand your situation better too.

Quality of Time Matrix

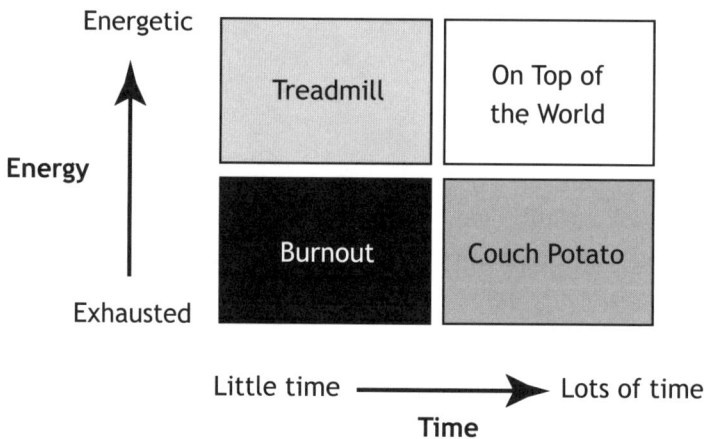

Burnout:
Feeling very low in energy and having very little time for doing things that are important to you.

Couch Potato:
Feeling very low in energy but having lots of time at your disposal for doing things that are important to you.

Treadmill:
Feeling full of energy but having very little time for doing things that are important to you.

On Top of the World:
Feeling full of energy and having lots of time at your disposal for doing things that are important to you.

Excercise 5:   The Quality of My Time

To determine the *quality of your time*, record your responses to the following points:

- Identify two to three examples of activities you engage in when you are in each quadrant.
- Identify the overall feeling you have when you are in each quadrant.
- Next, estimate how much of your time you spend in each quadrant in a typical week.

Quadrant	Activities	Overall Feeling	Percentage of Time Spent
Burnout	_____	_____	_____
	_____		
Couch Potato	_____	_____	_____
	_____		
Treadmill	_____	_____	_____
	_____		

**On Top of
the World**

_____   _____   _____

_____

_____

Which quadrant most characterizes your life and your work right now?

_____

_____

_____

_____

Spending more time in the quadrant On Top of the World requires the desire and ability to say "no" to competing demands. To which demands would you like to say "no"?

_____

_____

_____

_____

What is the smallest step you could take that would move you in the right direction?

_____

_____

_____

_____

What other steps might you consider taking?

_____

_____

_____

_____

What Jennifer is learning, and what we all need to learn, is that it makes no sense at all to manage time without also managing energy. If Jennifer really wants to pursue a career in law, she needs to first find a way of reserving a little bit of time, and energy, to move ahead with her goal.

How can she accomplish this?

First and foremost, Jennifer needs to say "no" to some of her current demands. In order for this to work, she must be gentle with herself and courageous. Should she spend less time with her children? Should she give up her part-time job in the bar? Should she reduce the number of work hours in her full-time position? These are tough questions, and to answer them, she needs to respect her relationship with Self—who she truly is and what she really wants.

Often, the best approach is to make small changes, slowly. What is the smallest step she could take that would move her in the right direction? Perhaps it is exploring with her boss the possibility of company sponsorship for her training; asking a family member to assist in child support; phoning various law offices to see if she could do part-time work after hours, instead of her work in the bar; checking with her community college to see what financial assistance they can offer her; finding out if she can do the training she needs by correspondence; postponing her career aspirations until after her children are a little older...

Jennifer's courage paid off. After approaching her boss, she discovered that her company was willing to provide a small amount of paid work time for her to study as well as reimburse her for some of her training expenses if she maintained a "B" standing and was willing to work in their legal department for two years after graduation.

Since her company was willing to provide her with this kind of support, she was able to reduce her part-time hours from three days a week to an easier two.

It worked out. The key in Jennifer's case was to take small steps, slowly. Of course, some situations might not be resolved so easily. Jennifer might have needed to exercise different options. Still, it requires a great deal of courage to initiate a conversation about your personal situation and career aspirations—especially with your boss.

In order to more fully understand who you are and what you want, it can be very useful to analyze your present use of time in your work and also in your personal life, then compare this with how you would ideally like to spend your time.

As you begin to approach your ideal and you gain a stronger sense of priorities in your work and in your life, your sense of fulfillment, energy and enjoyment will rise. In addition, you can avoid the stern criticism that a professional coach once barked at one of his athletes. "Look!" he shouted, "You're either doing the right thing at the wrong time or the wrong thing at the wrong time!"

The following exercises emphasize the importance of investing your time and energy in the things that matter most to you. Time is precious. Be clear on who you are and what you want. Do the right thing at the right time.

Exercise 6: My Working Moments

Draw a pie diagram to represent how you spend your time at work.

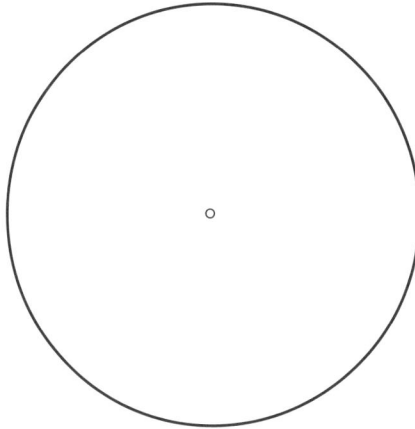

Here's an example of my own Working Moments diagram:

Exercise 7:   My Personal Moments

Draw a pie diagram to represent how you spend your time away from work.

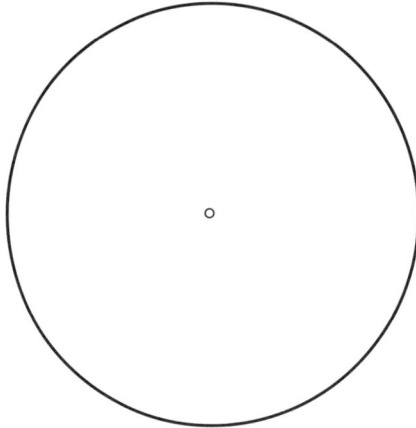

Here's an example of my own Personal Moments diagram:

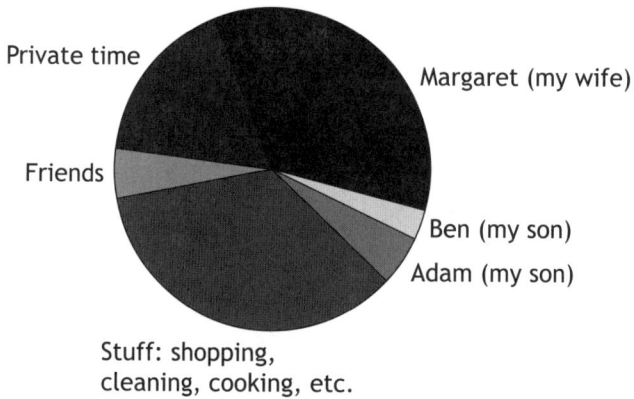

Private time

Margaret (my wife)

Friends

Ben (my son)

Adam (my son)

Stuff: shopping,
cleaning, cooking, etc.

Exercise 8:   My Ideal Job

Now draw a pie diagram to represent the ideal work situation for yourself. How would you like to spend your time in your ideal job?

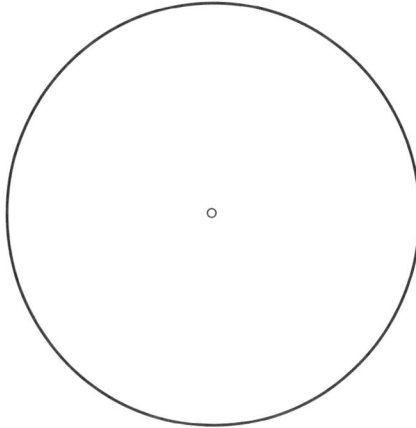

Here's my own Ideal Job example:

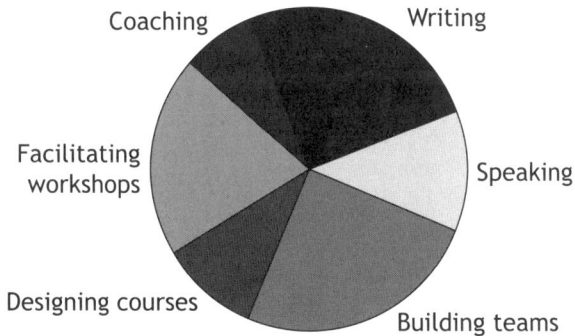

Compare your Ideal Job diagram to your Working Moments diagram. How different are they? How easy would it be for you to realize your ideal job?

Answer these questions:

What is the smallest step that you could take that would move you in the right direction?

_____

_____

_____

_____

What other strategies could you use to move yourself towards your ideal job?

_____

_____

_____

_____

Exercise 9:   My Personal Ideal

Now draw a pie diagram to represent the ideal situation for yourself away from work. How would you like to spend your time in your personal life?

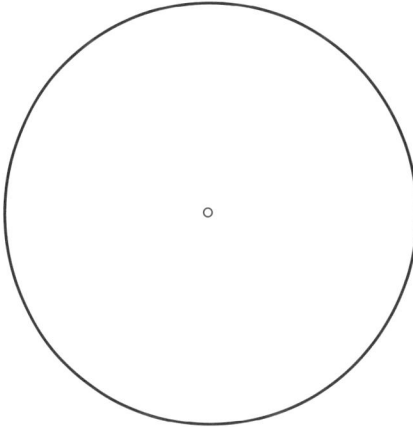

Here's my own Personal Ideal example:

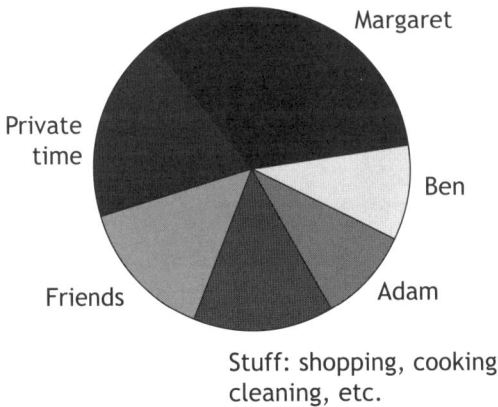

Compare your Personal Ideal diagram to your Personal Moments diagram. How different are they? How easy would it be for you to realize your Personal Ideal?

Answer these questions:

What is the smallest step that you could take that would move you in the right direction?

_____

_____

_____

_____

What other strategies could you use to move yourself towards your personal ideal?

_____

_____

_____

_____

Remember, time is life. How you choose to spend your time is how you choose to spend your life. Moreover, your investment of time is an outward reflection of your relationship with Self.

Don't just let the future happen. Participate.

Keep in mind that it is often wise to make small changes, slowly. Remember to ask yourself, "What is the smallest step I could take that would move me in the right direction?"

In the next chapter, you will see how the tendency to divide our lives into compartments of work and personal time can create unhealthy workplaces as each of us acts upon our notion of our work roles while parking our personal values, aspirations and feelings at the door when we go to work.

Ultimately, in order to enrich the time you spend at work, you need to act consistently with your personal values. So the next chapter will look at how you can bring more of who you truly are to what you do. In short, it will help you bring your work to life.

Personal Values:
What Values Would You Like
to Live by at Work?

Many of the interpersonal problems that are so often experienced in the workplace stem from the fact that people tend to compartmentalize their lives into two categories: work and personal life.

You have a personal life where you live the life of your *natural* Self. This is the Self that has grown out of your experiences with your parents, friends, teachers and community. It is from these experiences that you have developed your personal values, and your natural Self is the part of you that lives in accordance with these values. It is your nature.

You also have work, where you play a specific role, for which you are paid. Some people behave quite differently when they're playing their work roles than when they are at home and in their personal lives. They are actors on a stage. They try to appear natural while not being true to their real nature. They become their work roles—technicians, nurses, managers, engineers, administrators, operators, union representatives, team leaders, et cetera.

At work, personal values no longer apply. You are no longer your Self. Along with your colleagues, you play at being your notion of what your role entails. It's a kind of artificial life where oftentimes personal values, aspirations and feelings are left in the parking lot. After all, it's business, not life. You might not treat your friends the way you treat some of the people at work, but it's okay; it's expected. It's just part of the role.

Pierre is a director general in a small government agency. His agency is responsible for reviewing and resolving complaints about the city's public transportation services.

Today, Pierre is facilitating a very challenging meeting with his agency managers. They are all part of his direct staff, and collectively they must decide which one of them is to be laid off. The agency, as part of a larger government cost-cutting initiative, must reduce 10 per cent of its workforce, including management. Since Pierre has 10 managers, one of their positions must be declared surplus and the incumbent laid off.

Pierre didn't like the idea of having to do this. Nobody liked the idea, but all realized that it had to be done. His boss, the assistant deputy minister of Customer Service, told him to think about it over the weekend and then announce his decision to his staff on the following Monday morning.

Pierre didn't want to make his decision that way. It conflicted with an important personal value of his; that is, he always wanted to treat everyone with openness and honesty. So he said he would indeed think about it over the weekend, but on Monday he would hold a meeting to consult with his management staff before making his decision. His boss totally disagreed with this approach, but allowed Pierre to go ahead with his "hairbrained" scheme anyway.

The meeting covered a lot of ground. It reviewed and prioritized the entire range of services offered by Pierre's team. At the end of the day, it was becoming more and more obvious as to which position was most logical to be declared surplus. Pierre thanked his team for their participation through a very challenging and important meeting. He said he would consider the group's input and announce his decision the next day.

He then asked each manager to express their final thoughts and feelings about the meeting. Each one, without exception, expressed how happy they were to have been part of the decision-making process. They appreciated everyone's openness and honesty.

The last comment was reserved for Sharon, the manager whose position was most at risk. She responded, "I want you all to know that this has been a very difficult day for me. But I would really like to thank you for allowing me to participate in this decision. I really appreciate that it wasn't just made behind closed doors."

No one left that meeting in a hurry. People lingered. Sharon thanked Pierre personally and all nine of Sharon's colleagues spoke to her and offered their support before leaving.

Business is personal. It affects people's lives. How you choose to be, at work, affects all the people with whom you come into contact. Separating our lives into personal and work roles allows us to act one way at home and another way on the job, and this separation creates workplaces that are fearful, dispirited and unmotivated. There is an acute need today for people to more fully express their true Selves in their work lives. There is a need to bring life to the workplace.

How then do you bridge the gap between who you are and what you do? How do you live a more integrated and meaningful life? How can you be more of your *natural* Self at work? You will see in the next exercise that having a good understanding of your personal values can help bridge the gap between personal life and work life. And ultimately, acting in accordance with your values is the best way of truly being your Self at work.

Exercise 10: The Values I Would Like to Live by at Work

Take the time to think about how you can bring more of who you truly are to what you do. Pierre did this by sticking to his personal values even when things got tough. What values would you like to live by at work?

Using the chart on page 50, list three personal values that you would like to uphold for yourself while at work.

Next to each value, describe between one and three behaviors that you could use to bring that value to life. In other words, what do your values look like in action? Plan to engage in these behaviors consistently.

Finally, for each value, describe between one and three behaviors that you sometimes engage in that undermine the value. In other words, what do you sometimes do that gets in the way of upholding your values? Plan to reduce or eliminate these behaviors.

You might wish to use the following example as a guide.

My Personal Values	Behaviors that represent each value	Behaviors that undermine each value
Be honest.	Tell the truth consistently.	Skating around the real issue.
	Share as much information as possible with my staff.	Pretending I know the answer when I don't.
	Say "no" when I really don't want to do what someone is asking me to do.	Saying "yes" when I know I should say "no."

My Personal Values	Behaviors that represent each value	Behaviors that undermine each value
1. _____ _____ _____ _____ _____	_____ _____ _____ _____ _____	_____ _____ _____ _____ _____
2. _____ _____ _____ _____ _____	_____ _____ _____ _____ _____	_____ _____ _____ _____ _____
3. _____ _____ _____ _____ _____	_____ _____ _____ _____ _____	_____ _____ _____ _____ _____

Think of a specific work situation in which you might find it challenging to live according to the values you identified above.

_____

_____

_____

_____

What could you do to remind and encourage yourself to use the appropriate behaviors that represent your values in this situation?

_____

_____

_____

_____

What could you do to ensure you don't use the behaviors that undermine your values?

_____

_____

_____

_____

The distinction between work life and personal life, as we have observed, is artificial. You only have one life and part of it is spent on the job and part of it is spent outside of work. In order to bring more of who you truly are to what you do, you need to act in accordance with your personal values in all aspects of your life. This is an essential part of developing an effective relationship with your Self.

Furthermore, as you put your personal values into action, you begin to humanize your workplace. You become more "person-able." You begin to treat your colleagues, customers and managers as complete human beings and not merely as the personification of various work roles. After all, business _is_ personal.

In the next chapter, you will have an opportunity to consider your current work–life balance. Many people find it very challenging, if not impossible, to achieve the right balance between the amount of time and energy they invest at work relative to the amount of time and energy they invest at home. Moreover, the right balance varies from individual to individual, is not easy to achieve, and is quite dynamic.

Yet there is no use being rich in your professional life if you are bankrupt in your personal life. The next chapter will help you achieve your ideal work–life balance. This balance is essential to deriving meaning and motivation from work and realizing an overall healthy level of well-being and fulfillment.

Work—Life Balance

Ng-Lee is a very successful electrical engineer specializing in photonic technology. His wife, Gertrude, is a top purchasing agent for a large textile firm. Both travel extensively. For the past 10 days, Ng-Lee has been in England, France and Germany. Gertrude has been working in Singapore and Rome. This week, Gertrude flies home to Toronto while Ng-Lee wraps up his trip in Germany. When Ng-Lee finally lands in Toronto on Friday, Gertrude will be preparing his suitcase so that he's ready to leave for San Diego on Sunday morning.

Their lives have been like this for the past two years. It seems that the more successful they become, the more they need to travel and put extra hours into their increased responsibilities. They do in fact love their jobs, but both realize that their work—life balance is off kilter.

Both Gertrude and Ng-Lee would like to start a family. They feel they are neglecting their friends and they barely manage to see their parents once in a while. Moreover, their own relationship has become rather haphazard. They take each other for granted in spite of the fact that they do make a great team together. They realize that their teamwork mostly involves helping each other stay on top of their jobs.

Gertrude has been putting off beginning her studies in alternative medicine while Ng-Lee would be happy just to have the time to tend his gardens. Both miss simply going for walks together. They would love to be able to take a little holiday in the south, especially once the weather turns colder. Who knows, maybe they might even find the time to start a family?

Do Gertrude's and Ng-Lee's lives resemble yours? What does it mean to be successful? Being good at what you do is important, but it is also insufficient. There are people who devote their entire lives to achieving economic goals. They can amass great fortunes. They're smart and they work hard. They could even be well-intentioned and generous with their money. But if their personal lives are in ruin, if they don't have time to be with their families, get together with their friends, take time just for themselves…are they in fact successful? What is the use of being rich in your professional life if you are bankrupt in your personal life?

Life is one indivisible whole. To separate life into personal and work categories can do a great injustice. You need to consider your life in a holistic way. You need to be able to identify all the important pieces in your life and then put them together in one package. Then, as a package, consider your life. Do you have it together? Is your work–life in balance? Gertrude's and Ng-Lee's work–life was not. They decided to fix it before it fixed them.

As Gertrude is driving her husband to the airport Sunday morning to catch his flight to San Diego, she says, "Let's make our own long weekend when you get back and plan to spend it together, just you and me. What do you say?"

"Sounds great!" Ng-Lee sighs. "Let's do it. But," he adds sheepishly, "I really don't have time to plan it."

Gertrude smiles as though she's been thinking about this for a long time. "I know. Don't worry about it. I'll take care of everything."

Once the weekend arrives, Gertrude picks up Ng-Lee at Pearson International, and without telling him where they're going, she drives him north from Toronto to a beautiful resort on Lake Simcoe. This will be the venue for their long weekend together. It's beautiful.

After checking in, Gertrude hands Ng-Lee a portfolio. "Oh no," he frowns, "more work!"

"No," she laughs, "I made this just for you and me! I figured if I didn't make it look professional, you wouldn't take it seriously."

Ng-Lee finally takes in the title on the portfolio, "Create-a-New-Life Weekend."

Now he laughs as he opens the cover to scan the agenda for their weekend meeting.

"Very professional," he teases.

The agenda includes:

Friday	**Sunday**
Romantic dinner	Sleep in
	Our Ideal Year*
Saturday	Lunch
Breakfast in room	Boat tour
Bike ride	Our Life Is Poetry in Motion*
Our Life in Pictures*	Romantic dinner
Lunch	
Therapeutic massage	**Monday**
Sauna and swim	Sleep in
Dinner and dancing	Sauna and swim
	Our Moment of Truth*
	Begin our new life together

Ng-Lee is very impressed and wants to know more about the four items marked with an asterisk (*) on the agenda.

Our Life in Pictures:
Gertrude explains that they will make a collage together. She has brought some magazines, scissors, glue sticks and a piece of Bristol board for this. The collage will represent what they each want to incorporate most into their lives.

Our Ideal Year:
The ideal year exercise is intended to color-code a 12-month calendar in order to indicate how much time they would ideally spend on activities such as work, vacation, family, friends, personal development, et cetera. This way, they will actually be able to see their representation of their ideal work—life balance.

Our Life Is Poetry in Motion:
They will each write a poem. The poem is just for fun and is intended to summarize their feelings for each other and about their "Create-a-New-Life Weekend" together.

Our Moment of Truth:
This is the "decisions" portion of the agenda. It is the point at which they will choose which goals and changes they will incorporate into their lives over the next year.

Ng-Lee kisses Gertrude lightly on the cheek and says, "Thank you. This looks great!" He then grins and adds, "Can we schedule our next long weekend right away?"

Is your life as busy as Gertrude's and Ng-Lee's? What does success mean to you? Do you have time to be with your family, get together with friends, and take time just for you and your partner?

Of course not everyone is rich in their professional life or bankrupt in their personal life. Most people do not experience these extremes. For example, you might not consider your work experience to be rich, yet you enjoy your work and it pays the bills. Your time when at home might be busy with children and other responsibilities, but it's not bankrupt; it provides you with a sense of meaning and fulfillment. Moreover, you might not live in the traditional family setting of husband and wife with two or three children. Consider Frank and Claire, for example.

> Frank is 19 years old and lives with his mother. His father passed away several years ago and since that time he and his mom have become best friends. Frank is an only child and recently has been trying to stretch his wings. He studies as often as he can, works part-time, plays sports, and goes out with his girlfriend on Friday and Saturday nights.

> Meanwhile, Claire, Frank's mother, holds down a good job, travels a little for work, helps take care of her aging mother, and plays bridge twice a week in the evenings. Claire's main priority is to keep the home running. Frank's main priority is to get admitted to a good university by the end of the school year.

> Needless to say, Frank and Claire don't see each other very often! And this is a real shame because not only are they mother and son living in the same house, but they are also very close to each other in spirit. So it's a wonderful surprise for Frank when Claire tells him about the "Create a New Life" weekend that she has planned for the two of them.

It will give them a chance to renew their relationship, rekindle their spirits and talk about their future. It is also an important opportunity, since Frank is most likely going to go to university out of town. The weekend will give them a chance to sort through some of their feelings about this as well as plan how they will continue to foster a good mother-son relationship.

Everyone can benefit from calling a time-out from the "busy-ness" of life to reflect upon their work–life balance and plan for the future. You can do this as a family, with a partner or completely on your own. The exercises that follow will help you create a new life.

The way that Ng-Lee and Gertrude approach these exercises would probably be quite different from the way that Claire and Frank would approach them. So your approach needs to be unique, too. Vary the exercises accordingly so that you can gain as much value from them as possible. Find your ideal work–life balance.

Exercise 11: Our (My) Life in Pictures

This exercise will help you to create a vision of the kind of life you would like to realize with your partner. You can also do this exercise completely on your own, if you wish. Your vision should include symbols of your home, lifestyle, work, interests, values and aspirations. Follow these steps:

- Gather several magazines, a large piece of Bristol board, scissors and glue.

- Cut out pictures, words and phrases from your selection of magazines that symbolize your vision.

- Discuss these with your partner and decide which ones will be used in your collage.

- Place and then glue your magazine selections onto the Bristol board.

- Discuss the finished product with your partner and place it in a prominent location.

Exercise 12: Our (My) Ideal Year

It can be very helpful to see a month-by-month calendar for an entire year of your life. What would your ideal year look like? This can give you an appreciation for the balance that you would like to achieve between work and personal life, between private time and family time, between time for personal growth and time for pet projects.

This exercise is best done individually and then discussed with your partner. Look for ways of supporting each other and working through any conflicting ideas together.

- Begin by identifying which segments of your life you would like to include in your ideal year.

- Then, choose a color to represent each one.

- Finally, color in the calendar provided on the following pages, to represent your ideal year.

Here are the work–life segments and related colors that I chose for my own calendar. Perhaps they will give you some ideas as to how best to do this exercise for yourself.

Work-Life Segments

Work-Life Segments	Colors
Consulting Business	Blue
Writing and Speaking	Violet
Personal Development	Green
Family	Pink
Travel	Red
Winter Escape	Yellow

Work-Life Segments   Colors

_____   _____

_____   _____

_____   _____

_____   _____

_____   _____

_____   _____

_____   _____

January

Sunday	Monday	Tuesday	Wednesday	Thursday	Friday	Saturday

February

Sunday	Monday	Tuesday	Wednesday	Thursday	Friday	Saturday

March

Sunday	Monday	Tuesday	Wednesday	Thursday	Friday	Saturday

April

Sunday	Monday	Tuesday	Wednesday	Thursday	Friday	Saturday

May

Sunday	Monday	Tuesday	Wednesday	Thursday	Friday	Saturday

June

Sunday	Monday	Tuesday	Wednesday	Thursday	Friday	Saturday

July

Sunday	Monday	Tuesday	Wednesday	Thursday	Friday	Saturday

August

Sunday	Monday	Tuesday	Wednesday	Thursday	Friday	Saturday

September

Sunday	Monday	Tuesday	Wednesday	Thursday	Friday	Saturday

October

Sunday	Monday	Tuesday	Wednesday	Thursday	Friday	Saturday

November

Sunday	Monday	Tuesday	Wednesday	Thursday	Friday	Saturday

December

Sunday	Monday	Tuesday	Wednesday	Thursday	Friday	Saturday

Exercise 13: Our (My) Life Is Poetry in Motion

This exercise is intended to be fun and creative. Ideally, it will allow you to delve into some of the deeper feelings you have for your partner and your experience of sharing these exercises together. Alternatively, you could also focus your writing on your feelings for your Self—or on your feelings for any other loved one in your life right now.

Keep in mind that not everyone is a writer, not everyone is a poet, but we all have feelings, and to that extent we all have poetry inside us. Follow these steps:

- Begin with five or ten minutes of continuous writing about your feelings for your partner and/or sharing these exercises with each other.

- Next, select those words and phrases that best describe the essence of what you would like to communicate to your partner.

- Using the words and phrases you have selected, compose your poem and share it with your partner.

For inspiration, here are two of my own poems. The first was written for one of my sons, the second for my wife.

Child's Song

You came from a seed
Like a flower
You don't even know
Where you've been
I wonder at times where you're going
Like a leaf afloat on a stream

You sprang to life
Like a fountain
Your eyes and ears
Opened wide
I know you're not mine forever
Like a cone from the tall lone pine

You'll walk this earth
Like a pilgrim
Discovering many new things
I hope you find
What you're after
Like a bird when it finds its wings

You lie in wait
Like a kitten
In this picture
Of so long ago
I hope I can share
In your journey
Like the bank in the river's flow

Long Will I Love You

Long will I love you
Through the soft sweet sound of rain
Through the winding hue
Of emerald dew
Until the sun comes out again

Long will I love you
Through every spangled night
Of glistening dreams
And diamond streams
Until the stars fade from sight

Long will I love you
Through tall waves of summer grass
Of ruby lace
And jet black face
Until the poppies bloom and pass

Exercise 14: Our (My) Moment of Truth

It's now time to make some decisions. Answer the questions below:

What goals could you formulate that would move you towards the vision that you created in your collage?

_____

_____

_____

_____

What could you do that would help you achieve the kind of work–life balance that is represented in your month-by-month calendars?

_____

_____

_____

_____

How can you best live the feelings and values that you wrote about in your poems?

_____

_____

_____

_____

Discuss your answers and agree upon between one and three goals that would help you move forward. If your lives are particularly busy, you might find it helpful to consider what the simplest goal is that you could reach easily.

Our (My) Goals:

1. _____

_____

_____

_____

2. _____

_____

_____

_____

3. _____

_____

_____

_____

Finding time to be with your family, get together with friends, share quiet moments with your partner, or simply be by yourself can be challenging. Yet these aspects of your life are just as important as the work you do in order to live a happy, meaningful and successful life.

Life is one indivisible whole. You cannot do well in one part of your life while ignoring another and expect to have a fulfilling life. You need to be able to identify all the important pieces in your life and then put them together in one package. This is the only way of creating integration in your life and achieving the right work–life balance.

You've now set some goals and taken the first steps towards creating your future. This is essential to establishing an effective relationship with Self. Don't just let the future happen. Participate.

Work and life are precious resources, and in the next chapter you will see how important it is to take care of your resources. Have you ever considered your Self as a resource, for example? You might even agree that it is a good idea to take care of your Self, but what is it, exactly, that you are taking care of? What does the Self consist of? And how do you take care of it? For many people, unfortunately, taking care of their Selves is an afterthought.

The next chapter will begin by defining what a "Self" is and then go on to describe how best to take care of this essential resource.

Body, Mind and Spirit

You're sitting in the plane, getting ready to leave the gate. As you taxi out to the runway, the flight attendant explains the various safety procedures for take-off. Amongst other instructions, you are advised, if an emergency supply of oxygen should become necessary during the flight, not to panic. An oxygen mask will automatically be released from the panel overhead.

You are traveling with a small child. In an emergency situation, whose mask would you put on first—yours or the child's?

Many people would first come to the aid of the child. But according to airline safety procedures, this would be the wrong thing to do—as heartless as it might sound. You see, if you don't take care of yourself first, then you won't be in a position to help another and you put both yourself and the child at risk.

This is, of course, a life lesson. You can only help others to the extent that you help yourself. Being there for others when they most need you depends a great deal upon your being there for yourself when *you* most need you.

However, believing that it is a good idea to take care of your Self raises an interesting question. What exactly is it that you are taking care of? What is a Self? Philosophers, theologians and others have grappled with this question for centuries.

Most people would agree that the Self is made up of at least three components: body, mind and spirit. These components serve as your personal resources. They define who you are. They are what you bring to work each day.

When these three aspects of your Self are well developed, then you apply the best of you to what you do. In a sense, this is a prerequisite for working effectively. Until your body, mind and spirit are well developed, *you* are simply not showing up at work. You're not all there.

Your Self

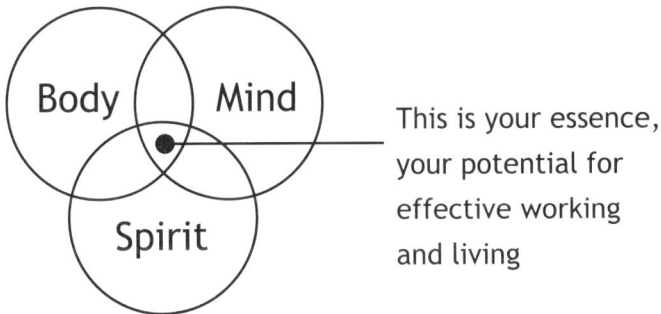

This is your essence, your potential for effective working and living

These resources of body, mind and spirit can be pictured as three circles moving through time. When body, mind and spirit are well developed, the circles are large, like well-exercised muscles. The area where the three overlap is the area of synergy and, ultimately, effectiveness. This is where you bring to bear all three resources, working together, in synergy with each other. The result is heightened awareness, clarity and insight. This center is the essence of who you are. It is your potential for working and living. It is your potential for finding meaning, feeling motivated and being productive.

Do you take these resources for granted? You might assume that your body, mind and spirit will always be there to serve you. Conversely, you might not even have the awareness of these aspects of yourself or think of them as resources in the first place. For whatever reason, imbalances sometimes exist, when one or more of the three are neglected.

All resources require maintenance. All resources can be developed. In this regard, body, mind and spirit are no different from your car, lawnmower or finances. Take care of them and they will take care of you.

Yet some people are too busy driving to take time to fill up the tank with gas. They cut the lawn with a dull blade. Or they overspend and wind up in debt. This creates weakness and imbalance in the system. One or more of your resources breaks or becomes weakened and unreliable. It begins to let you down because you have let it down.

Imbalance

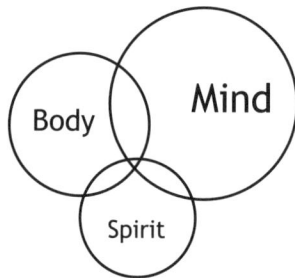

This diagram shows a typical example of imbalance. Many people tend to live in their heads—in their minds; they live from the neck up. They ignore, or take for granted, their resources of body and spirit.

The area of overlap or connection between the three resources then shrinks, leaving little room for synergy or for moments of awareness, clarity and insight. Much potential is lost. You're no longer bringing all of who you are to the table. You might be showing up at work, but you're running out of gas.

Relationships begin to suffer. You're just going through the motions. There are feelings of listlessness, apathy, even depression. In short, you feel empty.

To activate meaning as a motivator in your professional and personal life, you must first develop a good relationship with your Self. This requires taking care of, nourishing and exercising your three vital resources of body, mind and spirit. These resources are the central aspects of your Self. They are the basic components of who you are and what you take with you when you go to work.

The following exercises will give you some ideas about how you can best take care of these three vital resources.

Exercise 15: My Resources of Body, Mind and Spirit

Take a moment and draw three overlapping circles to represent how you see your resources of body, mind and spirit.

Then write a few comments in point form to explain why you drew your circles the way you did.

_____

_____

_____

_____

There are, of course, many ways to take care of and enhance your body, mind and spirit. Here are some possibilities for you to consider:

Body

Eat properly.

Get plenty of rest.

Exercise regularly (aerobic and anaerobic).

Groom yourself properly.

Take bubble baths.

Go for regular therapeutic massages.

Visit your health practitioners regularly.

Play.

Go for walks.

Take the stairs instead of the elevator.

Mind

Get enough sleep.

Exercise.

Take training courses.

Read professional journals.

Research subjects of interest.

Surf the net.

Play games like chess.

Read a good book.

Discuss subjects of interest with friends or colleagues.

Set challenging and meaningful objectives.

Spirit

Pray.

Read uplifting books.

Go for a walk in nature.

Develop relationships with friends and family.

Meditate.

Do random acts of kindness with no expectation of reward.

Do something to help someone.

Phone home.

Go to church, synagogue, mosque or temple.

Find ways to celebrate diverse cultures.

Notice that many ideas, such as "go for a walk," "play" or "get plenty of rest," could apply to all three resources of body, mind and spirit. In fact, any resource you choose to work on will inevitably affect and involve the other two. Pull on any flower in the garland and the rest of the garland will come along with it. You are a unified whole. For the purposes of analysis, it is necessary to dissect the Self into body, mind and spirit; in reality, they are inseparable.

Exercise 16: Taking Good Care of My Self

Now create your own list of the best ways to take care of your Self.

Keep in mind that this needn't be a chore. It needn't necessitate the creation of an endless TO DO list. Choose only those activities that you can imagine yourself truly enjoying and benefiting from.

Perhaps these ideas are activities that you are already doing. If so, keep them on your list.

Identify at least three ways of maintaining and/or enhancing each of your three resources of body, mind and spirit.

My Body

1. _____

_____

_____

_____

2. _____
   _____
   _____
   _____

3. _____
   _____
   _____
   _____

My Mind

1. _____
   _____
   _____
   _____

2. _____
   _____
   _____
   _____

3. _____
   _____
   _____
   _____

My Spirit

1. _____
   _____
   _____
   _____

2. _____
   _____
   _____
   _____
   _____

3. _____
   _____
   _____
   _____

As we have seen, most people agree that the Self is made up of at least three components: body, mind and spirit. These components represent your personal resources. When these three resources are well developed and maintained, then you apply the best of you to what you do.

In the next chapter, you will see that these precious resources enable you to bring a tremendous amount of consciousness and presence to each moment. Consciousness, in turn, creates meaning. When you are fully present, there are no longer any *un*meaningful moments. Ultimately, you can transform any event into a significant experience. You can bring your work to life.

Being There

John is an organization development consultant. Years ago, he attended a month-long training program on group dynamics. There were about 50 people attending the program.

During the second week of the program, he entered the training room where, just like every morning, a lot of students had already begun taking their places. On the way past Julie, a fellow student, he simply said, "Good morning," while touching her lightly on the shoulder.

Two weeks later, at the end of the program, the program participants were each asked what they felt the most significant aspect of the program was for them.

With tears streaming down her cheeks, Julie described the morning when John came into the room and acknowledged her with that light touch of his fingers on her shoulder. It was a moment that couldn't have lasted more than a second, but out of a four-week program, that moment was, for her, the most significant.

You see, Julie had felt lost and invisible until that moment. It was a turning point for her. At that precise moment, she brought the full force of her awareness to John's empathetic gesture. She transformed it from a trivial, chance encounter into a significant moment of intense meaning. Her consciousness created that meaning.

From that point onward, she revealed, "I was no longer invisible.

I felt 'noticed.' I gradually became an extremely motivated and involved participant."

The title of Peter Seller's last movie, *Being There*, is very telling. In order to create meaning in your work and in your life, you've got to *be* there. Mental focus creates reality. Consciousness creates meaning. When you are fully present, there are no longer any unmeaningful moments. When you bring your undivided, undiluted awareness to even the most apparently trivial events, you transform them into experiences of significance.

An essential aspect of developing an effective relationship with your Self requires you to be fully present, moment by moment. Be there.

The Creation of Meaning

Mental Focus		End Result
Conscious and Fully Present	$\Longrightarrow$	Significant Experience
Unconscious and Not Present	$\Longrightarrow$	Missed Opportunity

Consciousness and meaning form a causal relationship. The light of your consciousness shines through the dim clutter of everyday life and enlivens those elements that you select, making only those moments meaningful. Every moment is an opportunity for growth, every occasion is a special occasion, and every instant holds an eternity of possibility.

Have you ever been out driving, perhaps going to work, and upon your arrival wondered how you got there? You didn't so much drive the car as you were driven by the car to your destination. It was as if you were an automaton, driving by habit, or instinct, using automatic, unconscious reflexes.

Work and life can be like that. Some people are "being lived." They're not really living. You're at work, but you're on automatic, like cruise control; you're just going through the motions. What happens during those moments? What marvellous possibilities could materialize if you brought your awareness to them?

Consciousness is a choice. But there is a limit to how many pieces of information your awareness can handle in any given moment. Consciousness also represents an investment of energy. It's like juggling. How many balls can you keep in the air at the same time? Do you ever feel tired at the end of the day because you've tried to do too much? Try focusing your awareness on only one thing at a time. You can only actually do one thing at a time, anyway. You'll get more out of work and life that way. Less is really more.

Have you ever seen a shooting star? A beautiful flash of brilliance through a dark sky. But you've got to be there to notice it. You've got to be present in that moment to take in its rare beauty. Work and life are beautiful like that. Every moment is a shooting star. Every moment is significant. It is our awareness that makes them so.

Mohammed is a management consultant. He designs and delivers workshops to teach new managers basic management skills.

Five years ago, TLC Consulting Group asked him if he'd be interested in facilitating a one-day course for a government regulatory agency. Since TLC was already fully booked on the required dates, another consultant was needed. Mohammed agreed to provide the training but wanted to meet the client group first.

During Mohammed's meeting with the agency's senior management staff, it became apparent that a one-day workshop was not really an effective solution to the organizational problems that the agency was experiencing. A more elaborate and long-term strategy was needed.

Subsequent to the meeting, Mohammed submitted a proposal for the client's consideration. After some negotiation, a contract was agreed to. What started off as a request for a one-day workshop resulted in a five-year project.

Both the agency and Mohammed are extremely pleased with the outcomes.

How did a one-day workshop turn into a five-year project? When you bring the full power of your awareness to the moment, you see things that others don't. Mohammed saw something that TLC didn't see. He shared his insight with his prospective customer and it made sense to them. Your awareness is like a light. It shines through the dull morass of possibility. It illuminates whatever you choose to focus it on. It creates moments of meaning, moments of significance. These moments can enrich your work, your life and your relationships.

Consciousness creates meaning. Be there.

Exercise 17: Being There

Reflect upon your work life and choose an example of a situation in which you were fully present in the moment.

- Perhaps it was a situation in which you saw possibilities that no one else saw.

- Perhaps you were reviewing a piece of work and discovered something significant that otherwise might have been overlooked.

- Perhaps it was a situation in which you paid attention to your intuition and your hunches paid off.

Describe the situation:

_____
_____
_____
_____

What were the benefits of being fully present in that situation?

_____
_____
_____
_____

Using your situation as a reference point, what can you do to remind yourself to be fully present more often?

_____
_____
_____
_____

> **May you find joy in the moment**
> **And if it cannot be found,**
> **Be in the moment**
> **And let it find you.**

The secret to bringing your work to life is the exploration and development of three key relationships:

- your Relationship with Self—connecting with who you are and what you want;

- your Relationship with Others—connecting with people as individuals and as teams;

- your Relationship with the Higher Values—connecting with your own philosophy of life.

The first part of this book has focused on your relationship with Self. Developing an effective relationship with your Self is a prerequisite for working and living effectively with others.

In the next part of the book you will explore the second key relationship— your relationship with Others. This relationship is based on treating people compassionately, communicating with sensitivity and honesty, and making a conscious effort to transform your work group from a loose collection of individuals into a genuine community.

Remember, life is short—and at least half your waking hours are spent at work. So seize this opportunity to instill more meaning and motivation into your work. Develop the three key relationships. Bring your work to life.

Part Two

Your Relationship with Others

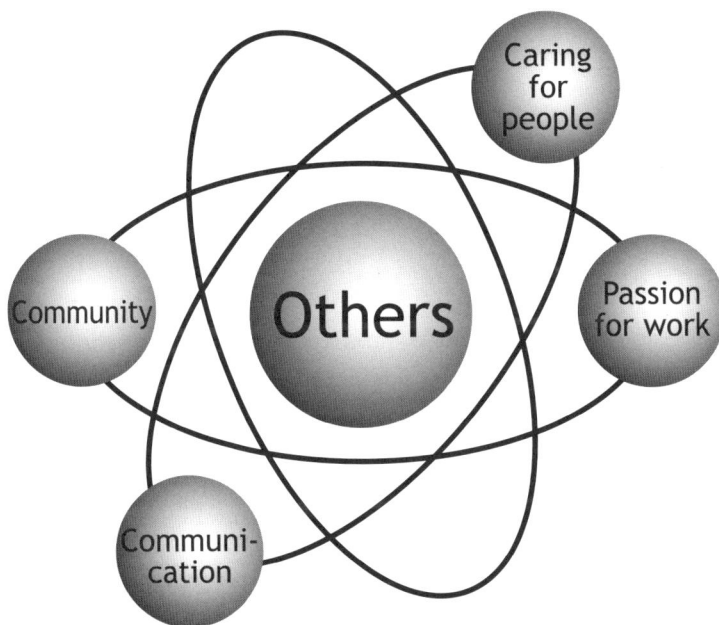

The secret to activating meaning and motivation in your work life is to develop three key relationships. In Part One, you explored the first relationship, your relationship with Self; Part Two will now highlight the second key relationship, namely, your relationship with Others.

Since you spend at least half your waking moments at work, your experience of work needs to be as meaningful as possible. Meaning in turn leads to personal satisfaction, motivation and productivity. Clearly, there are huge benefits for both the individual and the organization when individual employees find meaning in their jobs.

Some workplaces are mere collections of strangers. Others are teams—and while teams can be effective and productive, they too fall short of satisfying the need for meaning at work. The only way to satisfy the need for meaning at work is through the creation of genuine workplace communities.

Communities are characterized by compassion. This is how they differ from teams. Workplace communities balance a genuine caring for those who are involved in the work with a vibrant passion for getting the job done. The cornerstone of community is caring for people and passion for work: compassion.

Compassion emerges at the intersections of caring and truth, sensitivity and honesty, kindness and clarity.

Part Two redefines the term compassion, and transforms it into a very useful tool for building effective relationships with others. Part Two will focus on how to develop and nurture compassion in the workplace; how to communicate with sensitivity and honesty; and finally, how to transform an ordinary working group from a loose collection of individuals into an effective team, and ultimately into a meaningful, mutually supportive community where great things can truly be accomplished.

Caring + Passion = Compassion

• • •

Mark, Laura, Tim, Kathy, Alain and May Lee make up a small, but energetic, conference planning team for a non-profit organization. About a year ago, a group of 50 enthusiastic people decided that it would be a great idea to hold a conference on how to improve the quality of life at work. Once the actual work began, however, the group of 50 soon dwindled to a group of just six. In three months, they will run the conference, which includes over 30 keynote speakers and workshop leaders and more than 300 attendees.

The task has been daunting. None of the six conference team members has ever done this before. They have worked incredible hours. It has been physically and emotionally draining. So what keeps them going? They all believe in the task and are fully committed to it and to each other. Mark, as spokesperson for the group, has been asked many times, "Why are you doing this?" He has always answered without hesitation, "We are creating this conference because most people spend far too much time at work not to be fully alive while they are there. We need to instill and encourage more humanity in our workplaces."

Today, they are having a "catch-up" lunch at a favorite restaurant. This is a time when they catch up on each other's stories. Not a word is spoken about work. This is strictly personal. Sometimes the conversation springs up like popcorn—you never know who's going to say something next; and sometimes the conversation is structured—you are invited to react to a specific comment or question. But in spite of high volumes of tasks and tight deadlines, the conversation is never related to the work at hand.

Alain begins today's catch-up with the following: "It's really great to get a chance to connect with you all once again. I really look forward to these get-togethers, and I just thought it would be fun for all of us to share our answers to the question, 'What are you most looking forward to right now?'" With this, they each speak about their dreams, aspirations, hopes and goals.

This is what community in the workplace looks like in action. It means bringing your full commitment to the job because you genuinely believe in it, coupled with taking the time to check in with your colleagues about what you all have in common as human beings, not just about your work roles. It means working passionately on the task at hand, balanced with sharing and acknowledging each other's human journeys.

Other workplaces, however, are not so fortunate. They may become stagnant if there is little evidence of energy, commitment or passion for the job, and only superficial relationships between team members.

The members of some workplaces might be so absorbed in their own work that they have little time to acknowledge and relate to others. They immerse themselves in their work and are very productive, but they do not actively seek meaningful relationships with others. As a result, there is no sense of "team."

At the opposite extreme is the workplace in which some members are so busy socializing that their work suffers. Other people are forced to pick up the slack and animosity grows.

Obviously, balance is key. It is important to strive to create genuine community in the workplace by fostering and balancing passion for work with caring for people. The following matrix depicts four kinds of workplaces, each typified by a different key characteristic: Stagnation, Immersion, Socialization and Compassion. Which quadrant best describes your workplace?

Workplace Community Matrix

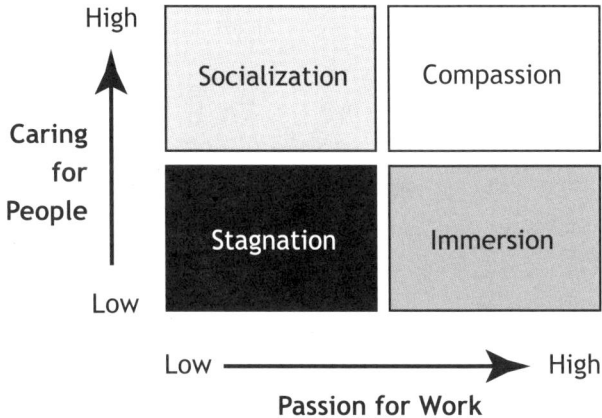

Here is a description of the four quadrants:

Stagnation:
In this quadrant, there is little caring for the people with whom you work and also little interest in the work itself. You probably feel listless, bored or trapped. There is very little work satisfaction and consequently very low levels of motivation.

Immersion:
In this quadrant, you are highly involved with the work you are doing, but hardly at all interested in the people with whom you do it. Here, there is little time to attend to others and a constant focus on meeting milestones and just getting the job done.

Socialization:
In this quadrant, the focus is on people. The work itself is secondary. The people with whom you work are really the reason you go to work. Socializing

rules the day. Getting the job done is not that important. The work is not compelling.

Compassion:

In this quadrant, you discover a sense of community at work. This emerges from the attitude, as well as the act, of working together to achieve a purpose that could not be achieved by one person alone. Here, there is a recognition of the importance of the job and the value of the individual. People are genuinely cared for and the work is conscientiously performed.

Each member of the workplace can make a contribution to developing community. How do you personally approach your job, for example? Think about your own workplace attitudes and behaviors. To what extent are you currently contributing to developing and nurturing a genuine community in your workplace? The following exercise will help you reflect upon these issues.

Exercise 18: Community in the Workplace

Answer the questions below:

In which quadrant would you place yourself as you currently approach your job?

_____

_____

_____

_____

What are 3 to 5 adjectives that would best describe your attitude and behavior at work?

_____

_____

_____

_____

What are the positive outcomes of your current approach to your work?

_____

_____

_____

_____

What are the drawbacks of your current approach to your work?

_____

_____

_____

_____

On a scale of 1 to 10, how satisfied are you with your current approach to your work? Circle the appropriate number below:

1	2	3	4	5	6	7	8	9	10
Not at all satisfied				Somewhat satisfied				Completely satisfied	

What could you do differently that would increase your level of work satisfaction?

_____

_____

_____

_____

What could you do differently that would have a positive impact on your workplace community?

_____

_____

_____

_____

Work represents a huge investment of your life. You spend far too much time in the workplace not to be fully alive while you're there. Work needs to become a meaningful experience, not just an economic necessity. Meaning in turn creates personal satisfaction, motivation and productivity. This is clearly beneficial for both the individual employee and the organization as a whole.

The only way to satisfy the need for meaning at work is through the creation of genuine workplace communities.

Workplace communities balance a genuine caring for those who are involved in the work with a vibrant passion for getting the job done. The cornerstone of community is caring for people and passion for work: compassion. In the next chapter, you will see how the power of the first dimension of compassion—caring for people—can completely transform your workplace.

Caring for People:
Learning to Love the People
with Whom You Work

Caring for people is one of the two essential dimensions of compassion, and compassion is the hallmark of community in the workplace. In order for community to be created in the workplace, caring for people must be present.

Caring can take many forms. It can show up as respect, integrity, trustworthiness, kindness or empathy. It really amounts to *love at work*. In this chapter, you will see how the power of love can truly transform your workplace.

Why do you work? There are many reasons people work. The most obvious reason is economic necessity. But even people who are financially well off go to work. Why?

If you examine your own reasons for working, you are sure to realize that one of the reasons is to experience community. Socialization is an important aspect of most people's need for work. And in this day of cocooning, you see independent consultants and the telecommuters returning to the traditional 9 to 5 workplace because they need more regular contact with people; they need the interactions of a team; they need a greater sense of community—in short, they need to love and be loved. Caring for people is an essential aspect of work. It is one of the main reasons that many workers consider their workplace a *home away from home*.

It is for this reason that competence has become the most overrated quality of our time. Knowledge, skill, technique and intelligence are nothing more than weapons in the hands of the person who lacks equal amounts of empathy, kindness, respect and compassion. Intelligence pales in the light of wisdom. Cleverness is nothing compared to integrity. Knowledge is useless without trust.

Human beings have a fundamental need to be loved. Even among less socialized species such as monkeys, when the young are given a choice between taking food from a dispenser or playing with a soft terry-cloth figure, they usually choose to play with the cloth figure. According to many experiments, the slightest hint of a loving parent has consistently won out over the need for food.

In *The Sacred Balance*, Dr. David Suzuki reports that since 1990, Americans have adopted over 9,000 children from Eastern European orphanages. Since many of the orphanages are overcrowded, the adopted children have often been deprived of human contact and love, and consequently have developed serious disorders, such as hyperactivity, aggressiveness, refusal to make eye contact, speech and language impediments, attention deficit and hypersensitivity to being touched.

Remarkably, however, since being placed with their new families, most of the children have either completely overcome their pasts and are thriving, or have at least made vast improvements. It therefore appears that if love cannot conquer all, it can at least conquer most problems.

In the workplace, the practice of love translates into treating your fellow workers with respect. This is an integral part of what is meant by *caring for people* and it is essential to establishing a genuine workplace community.
As you undoubtedly are aware, not everyone has a full appreciation of the need for love, caring and respect in the workplace.

Louis is a supervisor in a highly structured security organization. He works on a large base and is in charge of the maintenance of heavy equipment. One such piece of equipment is the JD3000, a one-and-a-half-ton tractor. Louis is an expert in keeping this piece of equipment running like a top. Before he became a supervisor, he spent months working on it. He could fix it in the dark.

Louis is a big, burly man, about six foot three, 260 pounds, with a gravelly voice. He has recently phoned Jeanne in the Human Resources Unit to ask her assistance in coaching his four men in how to maintain the tractor. No matter what he does or how many times he shows them what to do, they still can't seem to figure out how to fix it.

"These guys are complete idiots," Louis declares in exasperation. "Maybe it's the way I'm coaching them."

Jeanne agrees to help. She wants to set an appointment to talk things over with Louis, but he has an even better idea. "Why don't you come over to the old garage where we've taken the tractor and you can watch me in action?" suggests Louis. This sounds like a good idea to Jeanne and so she agrees to meet him there the following day.

Louis meets her at the door and leads her into the large open area where the tractor is parked.

"Okay, you clowns, get in there and get it started!" barks Louis.

Jeanne can see the looks of embarrassment and even fear on the faces of his four young employees. After a few minutes, Louis paints the air blue with more aggressive language. "Come on, hurry up! You guys would have trouble tying your shoe laces!"

Louis is yelling and mocking his men throughout the entire time that

Jeanne is there. "They've got to know who's boss," Louis confides in her. Then he says with a smirk, "Watch this!"

Jeanne, already feeling really uncomfortable, is about to witness even worse treatment of Louis's poor men. She watches as he physically hauls them off the machine by the collar, all the while yelling and ridiculing them, bodies flying in all directions.

Then to everyone's utter amazement, except Louis's, he tinkers with the engine for a mere 30 seconds or so, and starts it up. No one knows how he did it, but the tractor's running beautifully. Just like new.

Louis turns to Jeanne like the cat that's just come home with the mouse: "You see what I mean!"

Jeanne has her work cut out for her. She has witnessed first-hand how competent Louis is at the technical aspects of his job. The tractor is running beautifully. But naturally, she also realizes that Louis is tremendously blind to the impact of his behavior on the performance of his crew. Most likely, he is treating his men the way he himself has been treated. It's the perpetuation of the *school of hard knocks*. Jeanne needs to make him see the disadvantages of this approach. After all, every time the tractor breaks down, who has to fix it? And while fixing the tractor might bring Louis the warm glow of accomplishment, he needs to reconsider whether this should really be part of his job.

Louis's performance cannot be fairly assessed by taking into account only whether he gets the job done; rather, it must also take into consideration *how* he gets the job done. Both the tasks accomplished and the behaviors exhibited are fundamental to overall performance. And Louis, like everyone else, needs to be accountable for both.

When you juxtapose an individual's level of competence (task accomplishment) with their level of caring (behaviors exhibited), the following perform-ance matrix is produced. It suggests the four kinds of strategies that might be effective in dealing with various types of performance situations. Louis's per-formance, for example, would best be represented by the quadrant Uncar-ing/Competent: "Coach."

Performance Matrix

	Incompetent	Competent
Caring	Train	Promote
Uncaring	Remove	Coach

Here are the general management strategies required to address the kinds of performance issues illustrated in the matrix. Although they are described from a manager's point of view, they can be very useful for you in managing your own performance as well as in mentoring and working with your colleagues.

Uncaring/Incompetent: Remove
The individual in this quadrant has a severe negative impact on the work group. They do not get results in the job nor do they get along with others. It is possible that they are in the wrong position, way over their heads and under stress. Realistically, they may need to be removed from the organization and into a role that is more fulfilling for them.

Uncaring/Competent: Coach

This individual uses competence as a weapon. Their superior knowledge, skill and abilities, while significant advantages to the organization, are not easily made available to others. In most cases, organizations depend upon teams in order to get the job done. These individuals are not team players. They need to be coached on the importance of getting along with and caring for others. This might be a blind spot for them, and if corrected, could result in tremendous improvements to their personal as well as professional life. If they cannot learn to interact with others more respectfully, they need to be helped into an alternative role, either within or outside the organization.

Caring/Incompetent: Train

This individual possesses the philosophy and skill of interacting well with other people. They genuinely care about others. Unfortunately, they do not possess adequate abilities to get the job done. Perhaps they are in the wrong work role, or the goals of the organization are not closely enough aligned with their own goals. They need to receive formal or on-the-job training in order to improve their knowledge and skill to do the job. If their work can be improved, they could be a real asset to the organization, and also feel better about their own contribution. If they cannot learn to perform the job at a sufficiently high level, they need to be helped into an alternative role, either within or outside the organization.

Caring/Competent: Promote

This quadrant represents the ideal. Here, there is a good balance between caring and competence. This individual works well with others and is effective at doing the job. They could be promoted into a mentoring or leadership role in order to expand the scope of their positive influence on others.

It is essential to emphasize that the way one person is treated in an organization affects all others in that organization. There is a ripple effect. Managers need to treat their employees the way they would like their employees to treat their customers. Team members need to treat each other the way they would each like to be treated. It's the Golden Rule. You cannot treat even the poorest performer or the most insensitive person in a way that does not clearly reflect how you wish them and everyone else to perform and behave.

We are all connected to each other. If you mistreat just one person, you diminish all of us. When you treat someone with dignity, we are all the better for it. Therefore, your treatment of others needs to be consistently considerate, showing balance between caring and truth, sensitivity and honesty, kindness and clarity. This is compassion in action: caring for people and passion for work.

> *No man is an island entire of itself;*
> *Every man is a piece of the Continent, a part of the main;*
> *If a Clod be washed away by the Sea, Europe is the less,*
> *As well as if a Promontory were,*
> *As well as if a Manor of thy friends or of thine own were;*
> *Any man's death diminishes me, because I am involved in Mankind;*
> *And therefore never send to know for whom the bell tolls;*
> *It tolls for thee.*

> John Donne
> *Devotions Upon Emergent Occasions*

Exercise 19: Enhancing Team Effectiveness

Whether you are a manager or an individual contributor, take a moment to reflect upon one of the teams to which you belong. Which team members would you place in each of the categories listed below? What is the impact on your team of each placement? What strategies could be used to enhance effectiveness of the individuals as well as the overall effectiveness of your team?

Performance Category	Impact	Strategies
Uncaring/Incompetent	_____	_____
	_____	_____
	_____	_____
	_____	_____
	_____	_____
Uncaring/Incompetent	_____	_____
	_____	_____
	_____	_____
	_____	_____
	_____	_____
Caring/Competent	_____	_____
	_____	_____
	_____	_____
	_____	_____
	_____	_____

Caring/Competent

_____ _____

_____ _____

_____ _____

_____ _____

_____ _____

It can sometimes take great courage, commitment and effort to provide a colleague, an employee or a friend with the care they need. Sometimes people require *tough love*. They seem to want one thing but clearly need another. Take Ellen and Jerry's situation, for example.

> Ellen has been the manager of the IT (Information Technology) Group for a large computer manufacturer for the past 18 months. She has a highly productive group, whose members work fairly independently of each other because of the nature of their jobs.
>
> Recently she has become quite concerned, however, with the work habits of one of her staff members. Jerry has been working very unusual hours. He's always been a bit of a loner and an exceptionally hard worker, but his hours have increased off the scale. He usually comes in to work by about 6:00 a.m., and lately has been working very late. One Monday, for example, he worked until midnight, after having also worked both Saturday and Sunday.
>
> Ellen knows the project he is involved with is very demanding. Still, she cannot comprehend how someone could continue to work as hard as Jerry seems to be working. She doesn't feel he looks well at all. So one night she decides to work late herself, and observe—from a distance—what he's doing. All she notices is that Jerry sits in front of his computer screen, beavering away on the keyboard.

When he decides to leave at around 10:00 p.m., Ellen makes up her mind to follow him, discreetly, out to his car. From a good vantage point, and much to Ellen's dismay, she observes Jerry get into the back seat of his car, cover himself with a sleeping bag, and seemingly go to sleep.

The next morning when Ellen comes in to work, she checks the computer log to see what time Jerry got in. She's alarmed to discover that Jerry re-entered the building at 3:00 a.m. and is still at work when she arrives at 8:00.

Ellen decides to speak to Jerry immediately. He tells her not to worry—it's nothing; he's fine. She insists on asking if anything is troubling him. She wants to lighten his project responsibilities. He again resists her help and insists he's fine. Ellen won't give up that easily, though, and suggests he meet with an EAP (Employee Assistance Program) counsellor. He agrees but never follows through. He's beginning to look even worse. He's avoiding Ellen as much as possible and is becoming a little aggressive.

Ellen is not sure what to do. Her boss is in the United Kingdom. Ellen calls Security and has them de-activate Jerry's badge. He can no longer enter the building. With a security officer present, she lets him know this. He's quite distressed but insists he's okay.

The following week, Ellen discovers that Jerry has been working from his computer at home. She informs Security and they cancel his company computer account. Now, he is no longer able to work at all. He's still receiving his full salary. Ellen does not want to suspend him without pay. Jerry phones Ellen to ask her what would convince her to let him work again. She says he must meet with a counsellor. Jerry finally agrees.

It is soon discovered that Jerry is in the early stages of a severe nervous breakdown. He is clinically exhausted. There has recently been a tragic event in his life and he is in a stage of extreme denial, dealing with it by immersing himself completely in his work. He has become utterly overwhelmed.

Ellen showed an extraordinary amount of caring for Jerry. It took courage to confront him with the realities of what he was doing. Sometimes caring for people requires great courage and energy.

First and foremost, whether you work as an independent or as a member of a more traditional workplace, it is essential that you take good care of yourself. Sadly, there are precious few people out there who, like Ellen, are sensitive, caring and courageous enough to watch out for you.

Secondly, when you take concrete steps to show your colleagues how much you care for them, it not only enriches their lives, but it enriches your own life as well. It is through these gestures of human kindness that you can bring your work to life.

Exercise 20: The Courage to Confront

Consider your workplace.

Who, in the past, has had the courage to give you the caring and attention you needed?

_____

_____

_____

_____

What did they do for you?

_____

_____

_____

_____

What impact did this have on you and on them?

_____

_____

_____

_____

Who most needs your caring and attention right now?

_____

_____

_____

_____

How might you provide this?

_____

_____

_____

_____

If you were to follow through on this, what outcomes might be achieved?

_____

_____

_____

_____

Caring for people can sometimes seem like a scarce commodity in today's fast-paced world of work. Nonetheless, it is one of the two essential dimensions of compassion, and compassion, in turn, is the hallmark of community in the workplace.

Workplace communities enable people to derive a great deal of meaning and motivation from their experience of work. Communities promote authentic relationships and high levels of productivity. If you truly want to establish a real sense of community in your workplace, then fostering a genuine caring for people is absolutely essential. The power of love can truly bring your work to life.

In the next chapter, you will have an opportunity to develop the other essential dimension of compassion, namely, your passion for work. Passion for work goes hand in hand with caring for people in creating workplaces where people actually *want* to go to work.

Passion for Work:
Learning to Love What You Do

There is sadness and outrage when someone takes their life suddenly, but most people think nothing of it if someone fritters away their life piecemeal over many years.

What is the true measure of life? It's in how you choose to live, not in how long you live. Death will come soon enough—for most, too soon; for some, too slowly. Ultimately, though, death will take care of itself, so you need to take care of life.

Buddha said, "Your work is to discover your work, and then with all your heart to give yourself to it." If you are to experience living, not just aging, if you are to discover that there is life *before* death, you need to discover your work, and then devote yourself to it. Don't fritter your life away; discover your purpose and then act on it.

According to many workplace studies, over 75 percent of employees are unhappy with their jobs. In the mid-1990s, when the Canadian federal government downsized by 65,000 people, it was discovered that if a buyout package had been offered to any employee who wanted one, so many employees would have quit that their departures would have effectively shut down the entire government. Why are so many people dissatisfied with their work?

Marsha Sinetar wrote a wonderful book called *Do What You Love, The Money Will Follow*. Doing what you love can obviously make a huge difference to how you feel about work. Unfortunately, finding a way to make money doing what you love, or looking for the perfect job, is not always a practical option. In addition, there are many people who change their jobs numerous times throughout their careers in search of the perfect job and who, sadly, still manage to recreate the same unhappy circumstances in their new job as they had in their previous one.

So while it would be ideal to do what you love, keep in mind that when that's not practical, you can always love what you do. There just might be a way for you to discover your *work* within your existing job.

The question then becomes, how can you love what you're doing when you don't love what you do? Here are a few ideas.

Be purposeful. Reflect upon your purpose in life. Why are you here? What contribution do you bring? Arrive at a sense of purpose and apply it to whatever job you're in. Sure, there might be other jobs more closely aligned to your sense of purpose—look for those—but remember, your purpose can most likely be applied within the context of the work you currently do. Love comes not only from the job you do, but also from how you do your job.

Cynic Stew

Many workplaces have served up the following recipe for creating cynic stew.

In a saucepan:
- place one young and eager employee
- add enough work to completely immerse
- spice it up to create delectable expectations
- warm slowly to create the illusion of safety and comfort
- add a dash of something unsavoury
- stir in some tantalizing but empty promises
- mix until totally shaken
- devour before ready

Cynicism, anger, frustration, disappointment are all healthy and normal reactions to everyday life. But these are places to visit, not to live. Know when you're visiting and know when to move out. If you need help in moving out, the best mover is your sense of purpose. Focus on that. Be moved by that. Ask yourself the question, "In this situation, what do I need to do to act according to my purpose?"

Be response-able. A salesperson cannot control whether or not a prospective customer will buy. Only the customer can do that. A union steward cannot control how a manager will interpret a collective agreement. That is the manager's decision. Nor can a parent control the behavior of a child (especially a teenager!). Ultimately, it is up to the child. Therefore, you need to discern which things are truly within your control and attend to them only. Being response-able means attending only to those things to which you are able to respond. Let go of the end-result. You cannot control it anyway.

Be there. It is virtually impossible to be bored, frustrated or anxious if you are truly focused on the task at hand. These emotions are only possible by "double-tracking;" that is, by comparing what you're doing to what you think you would rather be doing, or by comparing how it's going to how you wish it were going. The solution is to stay focused. Love doesn't make comparisons. Place your single-pointed attention on what you're doing, at the time you're doing it.

Be the observer. It is also important to be able to stand back from the action in any situation. Instead of getting caught up in the heat of the moment, let the witness inside of you see what's going on, including your own role in it. Let this part of you provide you with perspective and self-awareness. You can then make better decisions. Love requires compassionate detachment.

Andrew is the chief financial officer for a large textile company with branch offices in more than 150 different countries. Today, he is holding a meeting with 40 of his comptrollers from around the world. The meeting has gotten off to a good start. Everyone seems to be enthusiastic about the company's performance and future prospects.

In the room, on a side table, there are stacks of company brochures describing the families of products that their textile firm designs and manufactures. During the morning break, Andrew overhears about 10 comptrollers vaunting the new product lines. They have obviously been taken by the product descriptions and the elegant portfolios.

Andrew looks concerned as he notices this and decides to broach what he considers to be an important issue when the meeting resumes. He knows he needs to proceed diplomatically because he does not want to dampen the obvious excitement he observed at break time.

He begins by saying, "I noticed some of you at the side table looking through our product brochures at break. I want you to know that I, too, am very excited about the prospects of these new products."

Then he cautions, "But when we start believing our own propaganda, we're in a lot of trouble. Be passionate, yes. But keep it in perspective. Be able to stand back from these brochures so you can see where we really are in being able to deliver on these new product lines. Develop enough self-awareness so you can see how the industry, our competition, our customers, and a host of other important factors impact our company—and these products. Be passionate; but detach yourself sufficiently from the lure of these brochures to be *prudently* passionate. That's our job."

Be accepting. Many people do not accept themselves. It is estimated that up to 90 percent of self-talk (how we talk to ourselves) is negative. If most of us talked to the people around us the way we talk to ourselves, we wouldn't have many friends.

Cultivate self-acceptance and then bring that acceptance to others in the workplace. No matter how insensitive an act might be, step back far enough so that you are able to see with perspective. See how the insensitive manager was treated as a child, as a student, as an employee, and as a supervisor. Develop enough perspective so that you can understand how someone could act that way. Love is being able to accept them for who and what they are. Given their experiences and their choices, they could not have acted otherwise. It is through the practice of acceptance that you invite learning and encourage change to take place.

Neale has been a sailor in the Merchant Marine for over 15 years. Early in his career, as an able seaman sailing out of Seattle, he worked on a tall ship called the *Sea Dream*. His first—and as it turned out, last—voyage on the *Sea Dream* was rife with conflict, antagonism and bitterness. This was largely due to the shipmaster, Captain Johansen, who was cruel, violent and drunk most of the time.

Unfortunately, the shipmaster took a dislike to Neale early on in their three-month voyage. To make matters worse, while at sea the shipmaster is god.

Neale is a very skillful seaman and quickly learned to keep a low profile, while focusing as much as possible on his work. In spite of his efforts, Captain Johansen took advantage of every opportunity to humiliate him in front of the rest of the crew. Neale became very disheartened and resentful at this unfair treatment. He tried to redouble his efforts of focusing on his work and just doing as good a job as possible. But nothing he did seemed to please the shipmaster. Neale was becoming bitter.

Fortunately, at about this time Neale was befriended by a shipmate who had sailed with their shipmaster on a previous voyage. He told Neale that at that time, Captain Johansen was just the first mate, and the captain he had been sailing for was his brother, Lars. They were Danish and had been raised in a very close-knit, seafaring family. Tragedy struck one night during their voyage. In pouring rain, lightning and heavy seas, first mate Johansen fell from the yardarm, and Lars was swept overboard and drowned while attempting to rescue his brother.

When Neale heard this, he recalled how Captain Johansen walked with a noticeable limp. It seemed that the captain had never gotten over the loss of his brother who had died while saving him. But Neale was absolutely stunned to hear that he, himself, bore a striking resemblance to the captain's brother. The resemblance, his friend said, was uncanny, all the more so since Neale was also of Danish descent.

From that moment onward, Neale looked on the shipmaster with different eyes. Captain Johansen still continued to berate Neale at every turn, but it never affected Neale the way it had before. Somehow in softening his view of the shipmaster, he hardened his defenses against his attacks. In becoming more accepting of the shipmaster's behavior, Neale was able to increase his own resilience.

Although Neale could have talked to the captain about his possible resemblance to Lars, he decided not to. Instead, he simply decided never to sail for Captain Johansen again.

Be your *Self*. Many people edit out their truth at work. According to a recent survey of 35,000 workers, 93 percent of the respondents admitted to lying regularly while at work. People are sometimes afraid that the truth, that being our *true selves*, might harm us or others. When you are not acting out of truth, you are acting out of fear—and fear can poison the workplace and increase emotional stress. Fear is the polar opposite of love. Learning to love what you do entails telling the truth. How much of your truth can you share today? How much of your Self can you reveal? Practice truth; act out of love. If you are not putting all of who you are into your work, then your workplace is not all it could be.

One day, according to an Eastern story, the gods decided to create the universe. They created the stars, the sun and the moon. They created the seas, the mountains, the flowers and the clouds. Then they created human beings. At the end, they created Truth.

At this point, however, a problem arose: where should they hide Truth so that human beings would not find it right away? They wanted to prolong the adventure of the search.

"Let's put Truth on top of the highest mountain," said one of the gods. "Certainly it will be hard to find it there."

"Let's put it on the farthest star," said another.

"Let's hide it in the darkest and deepest of abysses."

"Let's conceal it on the secret side of the moon."

At the end, the wisest and most ancient god said, "No, we will hide Truth inside the very heart of human beings. In this way they will look for it all over the universe, without being aware of having it inside themselves all the time."

There might be a perfect job for you. There might be a perfect job for each of us. It might even be possible for you to do what you love within the parameters of your current job. Perhaps not. But it is always possible to love what you do. You see, love, like truth, is already inside of you—no search required.

Exercise 21:   How to Love What You Do

Assess your current workplace behavior according to the six guidelines below. To what extent are you able to do the following?

1. **Be purposeful**: Periodically remind yourself about your purpose and put it into practice.

1	2	3	4	5	6	7	8	9	10
Not at all				Somewhat					Completely

2. **Be response-able**: Attend only to those things within your control.

1	2	3	4	5	6	7	8	9	10
Not at all				Somewhat					Completely

3. **Be there**: Stay focused on what you're doing at the time you're doing it.

1	2	3	4	5	6	7	8	9	10
Not at all				Somewhat					Completely

4. **Be the observer**: Avoid getting caught up in things so you can maintain perspective.

1	2	3	4	5	6	7	8	9	10
Not at all				Somewhat					Completely

5. **Be accepting**: Accept yourself and accept others for who and what they are.

1	2	3	4	5	6	7	8	9	10
Not at all				Somewhat					Completely

6. **Be yourself**: Share as much as you can about what you truly believe with others.

1	2	3	4	5	6	7	8	9	10
Not at all				Somewhat					Completely

Which of the above guidelines represents your greatest strength?

_____

_____

_____

_____

Which of the above guidelines represents your greatest challenge?

_____

_____

_____

_____

List between 1 and 3 things you could do to enhance your love for what you do:

_____

_____

_____

_____

Remember what Buddha said: "Your work is to discover your work, and then with all your heart to give yourself to it." Don't fritter your life away; discover your purpose and then act on it.

Moreover, look for ways to do what you love. However, should that prove to be impractical, keep in mind that while you might not be able to do what you love, you can always love what you do. There just might be a way for you to discover *your work* within the parameters of your existing job. It might be possible for you to discover your purpose and put it into action right where you are.

In the next chapter, you will see how your orientation toward the people with whom you work, and your orientation toward the work you do, are reflected in how you communicate. Which is more important to you—the people with whom you work or the work you do? Of course these factors are both important in getting the job done, but striking the right balance between your concern for people and your concern for work is essential. Has anyone ever told you, *It's not what you said; it's how you said it*? Well, the purpose of the next chapter is to learn how to communicate effectively and with compassion. It's all about applying the best of you to what you do.

Communication:
It's Not What You Say, It's How You Say It

Fundamentally, the workplace community emerges at the intersection of Self, Others and Work. This is the sandbox of life where adults go to play. And ultimately, sandboxes are small places. As large as some companies are, when you do your work you start to bump into the same people over and over again. Most of your relationships are not only important but are also long-term in nature.

Therefore, at a minimum, you need to know how to get along well with people and, ideally, how to flourish with them. That is what this chapter is all about—how to establish effective, long-term relationships.

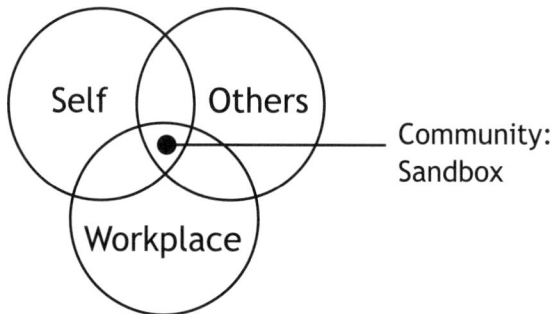

Self Others

Community:
Sandbox

Workplace

Establishing effective, long-term relationships requires that you learn to strike the right balance between your orientation toward the people with whom you work and your orientation toward the work you do. And this balance is reflected in how you communicate.

It's all about communicating with compassion. Remember, compassion represents both caring for people and passion for work. So, whenever you communicate, it's important to balance warmth with honesty, sensitivity with openness, and caring with truth.

Anna is the regional training officer in the Central Region for a large federal government department. Frank is the manager of the training function from federal headquarters. Although Anna reports directly to the regional director of Human Resources, she is expected to receive direction from Frank in headquarters, too.

After two days of meetings, Anna agrees to make certain changes to the way she reports training activities and costs so that the Central Region fits in more closely with the national reporting system that Frank is trying to implement. However, when Anna informs her regional management of the changes, her director quickly nixes them. Anna is extremely embarrassed, but sends Frank an e-mail explaining that the Central Region no longer intends to comply with his requests for standardization.

Frank explodes in his reply, calling Anna "inept and an obstacle to progress." Their relationship is stormy after that. About six months later, Frank decides he would rather be his own boss and so leaves his job to become a training consultant.

Two more years go by, after which Frank decides to return to his old department to bid on an important contract. The consulting business has been slow and Frank now finds himself in a situation where he badly needs to make money. The bidding has been close, but he is one of only two consultants being considered for the job. He is asked by the contracts officer to come in for an interview with the director of training.

Frank is feeling anxious and so shows up for his interview early. He hopes that will show how enthusiastic he is about the prospect of winning the contract. Inside, though, he is desperate. After sitting outside the director's door for the longest 10 minutes of his life, he is shown into her office. As he looks up to greet the new Director of training, he gasps and freezes in his tracks. It is Anna.

All relationships are long-term relationships.

Bruised relationships might not always come back to haunt you as they did to Frank. You might even say that it was just his bad luck that Anna was eventually promoted to director of training and ended up holding his fate in her hands. On the other hand, the world is a small place—a global village, as it is often called—and organizations are just microcosms of that little village. So can you really afford to brush off any of your relationships? Probably not. You need to treat all relationships as if they were long-term. They just might be.

Moreover, is there any one of us who doesn't deserve to be treated with respect? Is there any one of us who shouldn't be given the benefit of the doubt? Learn to look a little deeper. Remember Captain Johansen? Perhaps there is a story behind someone's bad attitude. How were they treated as a child? How were they treated as a student, an employee, a manager? Is it fair to treat them poorly because their need for compassion is greater than your own?

Dan works in an eight-story office tower that has a small cafeteria on the main level. Chantal is the cashier and, unbeknownst to her, is often referred to as "the troll." She makes no effort to acknowledge customers as they go through her cash; she doesn't smile or make eye contact; and she is often scowling, as if this were the last place on earth that she would like to be. That is, except when Dan goes through the cash.

Why is that? You see, some time ago, Dan took on Chantal as his pet project. She didn't know, of course, but Dan didn't think it was right for anyone to go through a major part of her life looking so unhappy. So he decided that in spite of Chantal's gruff exterior, he would smile at her, make eye contact, call her by her name, ask how she was and wish her a good day.

He persisted. And do you know, Dan is the only one whom Chantal smiles at, talks to and calls by name? It's as if they're long-lost pals.

When you treat even the most grumpy and nasty of the world with caring and kindness, you might become their only ray of sunshine for that whole day, week, month or year. It costs very little to be kind. Consider it a community service—because it is. It helps build genuine community at work. Consider also that, like all community services, you too might need it one day.

The most important aspect of communicating with compassion is that you know your intention. Being able to communicate skillfully is very much secondary to being aware of your motives in communicating at all. Skill pales in the light of intention.

You probably already know someone who is a very skillful communicator, but whom you do not trust. What good does it do you to be skillful, competent or knowledgeable if no one trusts you? Your character is far more important than your technique. Who you are is far more obvious to others than who you are attempting to portray.

So, before participating in any important communication, make sure you know your intention, and make sure that intention is honorable. If communication is a vehicle for exchanging information, then your intention is certainly the engine. In any communication, there are four possible intentions:

Express my truth with sensitivity.
Suppress my truth by withholding information.
Impress others by parading my knowledge.
Depress others by putting them down.

Vivian Marsh is the senior vice-president of Human Resources at a major international bank. She is the first woman to be promoted to a senior management position in the bank's history. Up until now, it has been very much an "old boy's network." The culture has traditionally been tough, risk-averse and hypercritical. Vivian was promoted to the upper echelons of this man's world because she was perceived to be tough and intelligent.

She was recently quoted in the local press as saying, "Most people here love the stress. They want to be stretched. And you do have to sacrifice things—like taking the kids to the hockey game. If the work pressure's there, then you'd better stay at work and get the job done. There has to be give and take—but usually it's a lot of give and a little bit of take. Those people who are unwilling to put their jobs before their families need not apply!"

Ironically, although Vivian oversees Human Resources, she is one of the most hated managers at the bank. She is intelligent but highly critical, and oftentimes her criticisms are personal. Moreover, she frequently laces her sentences with vulgar language and puts others down in public.

Unfortunately, Gary, one of her managers, took the brunt of her wrath yesterday morning. As he was stepping off the elevator in the foyer of the bank, she snapped at him over a report that he had rushed to write so that she would have it in time for an executive meeting. Because he hadn't had enough lead time to do the report, it was incomplete—although he had worked through the evening the night before.

In front of total strangers, colleagues and friends, Vivian blasted him so that everyone could hear: "Gary, you idiot, surely you know that this report is incomplete! Even a monkey could have done it better!"

Not wanting to make an even bigger scene, Gary slipped into the coffee shop with a couple of close colleagues, Nancy and Bernard.

Nancy is the first to speak. "Don't worry about her, Gary. Everyone knows she is absolutely detestable. She's an atrocious manager."

"Yeah," says Bernard. "She's the most hated person at the bank."

As Nancy goes off to buy the coffee and muffins, Gary looks over at Bernard and confidentially says, "This time I think I'll talk with my lawyer."

Communication Matrix

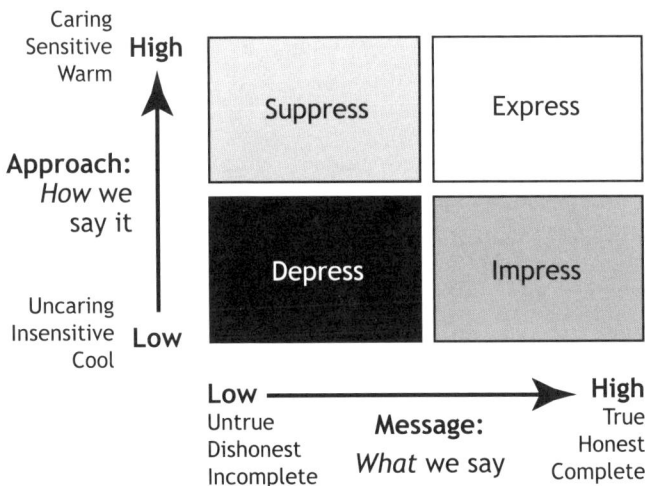

In the quadrant called **Depress,** the intention is to put others down. It is hurtful and unhelpful. It is vindictive and often takes the form of a personal attack. Here, the philosophy is that the best defense is a good offense.

The **Impress** quadrant is designed to dazzle others. It constitutes showing off. It is very much connected to and driven by ego. It can also take the form of an attack, or it can merely be insensitive and self-absorbed—looking out for number one.

The **Suppress** quadrant represents hiding your truth in whole or in part. Although it may be motivated by an unwillingness to hurt others, it is deceitful and misleading. Sometimes this takes the form of patronizing others or avoiding issues with them. It can also feel like "walking on eggshells" in our effort to avoid talking about certain subjects with certain people.

In the quadrant called **Express** the intention is to disclose your truth with sensitivity and warmth. It can provide opportunities for personal and mutual growth. It is the quadrant of caring and courage, and encourages the possibility of synergy and co-creation.

While it is sometimes tempting to depress others by putting them down, impress others by parading your knowledge, or suppress your truth by withholding pertinent information, there is a price to pay.

All relationships are long-term relationships. You never know who is going to come into your life again. And you never know with certainty the consequences of your actions. So why take chances in the way you treat other people? It makes good sense to treat others respectfully. It makes good sense to treat all relationships as if they were long-term—they just might be.

Therefore, always communicate with compassion. Compassion means finding the right balance between your concern for treating people respectfully and your concern for getting your work done.

To accomplish this, first and foremost, you need to know your intention before you communicate—and make sure it is honorable. Being mindful of your intention ensures that you are able to balance warmth with honesty, sensitivity with openness, and caring with truth. This way, you will always find the right balance between *what* you say and *how* you say it.

In the next chapter, you will see how you can use compassionate communication to transform your workplace from a mere collection of strangers into an effective team, and ultimately, from an effective team into a genuine workplace community where great things can truly happen.

Workplace Communities

You live in a time when most workplaces emphasize the importance of developing greater and greater levels of competence, knowledge and skill; a time when technique, technology, personality and appearance are given top priority. But who is the person behind the competence, knowledge and skill? Who is the user of the technique and the technology? Who is the person, standing right in front of you, whose personality you experience and whose appearance you see? Who are you, not as a work role, but as the authentic human being fulfilling that role? When your understanding of your colleagues moves beyond a mere knowledge of roles and appearance, then you begin to make the shift toward real understanding, appreciation and meaning at work.

In this chapter, you will learn how to transform your workplace into a meaningful, mutually supportive community where great things can truly be accomplished. Meaning requires revelation. Revelation requires respectful listening and response. In order to derive real meaning from your experience of work, you need to feel free to be your Self; you need to feel safe in revealing who you truly are and what you truly think without fear of reprisal. Your revelations need to be met with respect, genuine listening and response. The only way to achieve this level of meaning is by balancing caring for people with passion for work, resulting in compassion, the cornerstone of community.

Additionally, the members of genuine workplace communities share the myriad aspects and events of life's universal journey with each other. These events represent the human experiences that all people have in common, that you encounter in your own unique way. Yet most people are taught not to bring their personal lives into the workplace, and if you follow this advice, you ultimately become a two-dimensional character, the personification of a work role, and not a complete human being. The irony is that you share your personal experiences only with those who are already personally closest to you, keeping those who are not so close forever at a distance.

Communities are created through genuine dialogue: increasingly deeper levels of revelation and honest, non-judgmental response. The outcomes are closeness, cohesion, mutual understanding, respect, dignity and empowerment.

In this chapter, you will learn how to transform your workplace into a meaningful, mutually supportive community where great things can truly be accomplished.

> **When someone loves you, the way they say your name**
> **is different. You know your name is safe in their mouth.**
>
> **Billy, age 4**

Fiona is the manager of Product Verification for a large telephone company. This morning she is meeting with Ivan, one of her staff, to review his quarterly performance appraisal. Although the company does not require such frequent performance review meetings, Fiona likes to keep up-to-date with each of the members of her team.

In this past quarter, Ivan's work performance has trailed off and there are one or two significant concerns that Fiona will need to address. Overall, however, Ivan's performance is still all right. In fact, he is one of the most upbeat and friendly people on her team. Everyone regards him highly for his positive attitiude.

As Ivan walks into the conference room to meet with her, whom does Fiona see? Does she see Ivan, her senior testing specialist? Does she see Ivan who has been a work colleague for the past 12 years? Does she see Ivan the guy who has a bit of a performance problem right now? Does she see Ivan who lent her his pick-up truck a couple of years ago? Whom exactly does she see? Of course, to be an effective manager, Fiona needs to be able to take in all of these facets of Ivan. In order to be a compassionate human being, she needs to be able to do this, too. You see, being effective as a manager and being compassionate as a human being are pretty much the same thing.

Let's consider a snapshot of Ivan right now. Here's what he's been up to in the past few months. Here's who he is—and who Fiona needs to see.

Ivan:
— Is 52 years old.
— Takes medication for clinical depression.
— Has been the single father of two high-school-aged daughters, and has recently remarried.
— Has just moved into a new house with his wife and family.
— Has a brother who has been diagnosed with cancer this past year.
— Is in the process of helping his 80-year-old mother move out of her house where she has lived for the past 60 years and into a senior's apartment.
— Lives in a country whose economy is in recession.
— Works for a company that has implemented four rounds of layoffs this past year.
— Has never been the top performer in his work group, but has always been reliable and good-natured.
— Is nervous about seeing his manager because he knows his performance has trailed off this quarter.

— Is excited about going to a hockey game tonight.

This is who Fiona is seeing this morning. And, although Ivan's human journey is not much different from anyone else's, knowing it makes Fiona's picture of him more complete. Having a more complete picture of him makes it easier for Fiona to be compassionate: caring about Ivan as an individual and passionate about getting the job done.

In order for Fiona to see Ivan for who he truly is, she needs to create a work environment where Ivan feels free to be himself, an environment where he feels safe in revealing who he truly is without fear of judgment, criticism or reprisal. The only way to do this is through the creation of a genuine workplace community, the cornerstone of which is caring for people and passion for work: compassion.

To be effective as a manager and to be compassionate as a human being, Fiona needs to be able to balance her caring for him as a person with her passion for getting the job done. She needs to be able to see Ivan as more than a two-dimensional personification of a work role, and see him as the complete human being that he truly is.

Fiona does not need to solve Ivan's problems for him. He already knows that most of his current problems are life issues—ongoing and challenging, and issues with which he, like everyone else, must learn to cope. On the other hand, she can listen to him as he reveals as much about his situation as he is comfortable in revealing. She can then respond, in an honest and non-judgmental way, what she has heard and felt him say.

The benefits of her genuine dialogue with Ivan will be increased closeness, cohesion, mutual understanding, respect, dignity, empowerment, productivity and, ultimately, community. Holding Ivan accountable for his performance, as

Fiona undoubtedly needs to do, is much easier and more effective in an atmosphere of trust and safety. You see, being effective as a manager and being compassionate as a human being are pretty much the same thing.

Are you interested in developing a sense of community in your team? If so, the next exercise is an easy place to start. It will provide you and your colleagues with a simple and structured way of experiencing honest revelation and non-judgmental response.

Exercise 22:   Developing Community at Work

At a team meeting, in order to develop community and deepen your understanding of other team members, ask everyone to get together with a partner to discuss their thoughts and feelings about your workplace right now. The instructions for the exercise are as follows:

Revelation:
You have three minutes to reveal to your partner how the changes you have seen happening in your workplace have been affecting you personally (i.e., physically, mentally, emotionally, socially and/or spiritually.) The intention of the exercise is NOT to make you feel uncomfortable but rather to provide you with an opportunity to reveal as much as you can about your true Self—your thoughts and feelings.

Response:
At the end of this three-minute period, your partner will reflect back to you what they heard and what they *felt* you said—the true essence of your communication. Keep in mind that oftentimes the most significant part of the message is non-verbal.

As you reflect back to your partner, do not talk about your own feelings and opinions. The idea is just to capture and feed back the essence of what your partner said. This period of reflection will last approximately three minutes, too.

Once this is completed, switch roles and follow the same steps again.

After completing this portion of the exercise, address the following questions in the large group:

How did it feel to reveal your true feelings and opinions to your partner?

How did it feel to reflect back to your partner what you heard and *felt* they said—without adding in any of your own feelings and opinions?

• • •

Teams do not differ from communities in kind but rather in degree. Both teams and communities balance concern for people with concern for work. Both demonstrate compassion. However, communities delve much more deeply than teams into both the human and the task components of work. The members of workplace communities are completely focused and engaged in playing in the sandbox. As some authors phrase it, they are in the "zone."

They experience their colleagues and their work in very profound ways. Their work provides them with an opportunity to exercise their purpose for being on planet Earth. Their work allows them to put their calling into practice. Their work might not be their life, but it is their passion. Their work is not a waste of time, but a gift of time. Their work is not a pastime, but a pursuit. They bring their life to work, thereby bringing their work to life. They are not dead on their feet. They are not the walking wounded. They are just as fully alive at work as when they are at home. They are vigilant about their needs and strive to maintain a healthy work–life balance.

The members of workplace communities also experience their colleagues in very profound ways. They do not treat people in the workplace as mere personifications of various work roles. Their colleagues are not just two-dimensional shadows traipsing across the stage. Rather, they are genuine people with multiple dimensions, and many of them are friends. Members of workplace communities see others as having aspirations, needs, desires, dreams, hurts and fears. These human aspects are not hidden from view. They are cherished as part of being an authentic human being.

> **Love is when you tell someone somthing bad about**
> **yourself and you're scared they won't love you anymore.**
> **But then you get surprised, that they love you even more.**
>
> Matthew, age 7

Workplace Communities Model

You will see in the Workplace Communities Model on the next page that there are three dimensions. Both teams and workplace communities share a common concern for the two dimensions, Caring for People and Passion for Work. Therefore, the real differentiator between teams and communities is that the members of genuine workplace communities disclose much more of who they really are with each other. What's more, this kind of information is truly valued, cherished, even celebrated. Thus workplace communities are more deeply human and reach much higher levels of perspective than do ordinary work teams.

Open and honest

Revelation

Guarded
_____
Genuine

**Caring
for
people**

Uncaring
_____
Unmotivated ➤ Enthusiastic

**Passion
for Work**

Workplace
Community

Team

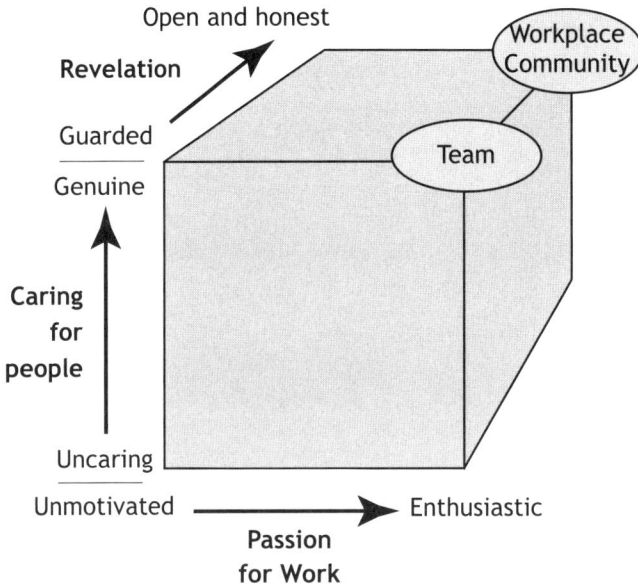

Finally, compassion in the workplace doesn't necessarily consist of being serious all the time. Compassion is also characterized by play, fun and spontaneity. As you relax into an atmosphere of acceptance, trust and caring, your childlike qualities of playful creativity and just plain fun emerge. Like children playing in a sandbox, you and your co-workers will experience how the energy and enthusiasm of fun stimulates and complements the drive to get the job done. Genuine workplace communities are fun places to work.

Jacques, Julie, Clare and Sandra are sitting around the table at a recent Chamber of Commerce event. They're chatting playfully about whose organization is the most fun to work for.

Jacques says, "I work at a large computer company and the enormous size of our campus makes it difficult to create any sort of community atmosphere, so we recently purchased a pool table for our immediate work area. It's really helped a lot. We work all kinds of crazy hours and this really helps to give people a place to gather and feel at home."

Julie, who works for a large federal government department, adds, "That's great, Jacques. I don't think we could ever justify that kind of purchase using public funds, though. We need to be a bit careful about perceptions. But we do manage to get together every month for breakfast chats. Our director picks up the tab for breakfast and we really do enjoy catching up on each other's stories. Sometimes we talk shop, but that's not really the reason for getting together. It's just fun."

"I agree," says Clare. "Our company is pretty small, about 23 technicians and a handful of office types. I don't know if I should tell you all this because you'll probably want to visit me every Friday afternoon. You see, every Friday around 3:00 p.m., the whole group meets in our lunchroom for a pub meeting. That's right, a pub meeting. We have a special fridge with a couple of handles sticking out of the door and two kinds of beer on tap. Everyone's allowed to have one brew, and we all just talk and have a great time. It's a nifty way to end the week."

"Well, it will be hard to top all of those great examples," admits Sandra. "Let's see. Well, this is quite different, but you know, it really is a great example of having fun. We're a small database management consulting firm, and as you can probably guess, most of our staff works on computers. So, a little while ago, one of our programming heroes got hold of the photos we took at last year's family picnic. That was a lot of fun, too, by the way. Anyway, he sorted and digitized over a hundred of these photos and made screen savers out of them. Over the weekend, he loaded them onto everyone's computer so on the Monday when we all came in, everyone began to see all of these pictures. It was fantastic. A really nice thing for him to do."

How much fun to work for is your organization? Do you have a pool table in your work area? Do you get together with your colleagues for breakfast once in a while? Do you have a *pub* day? Do you and your colleagues surprise each other with thoughtful and playful ideas? The next exercise will give you an opportunity to consider how you might energize your workplace through fun, play and spontaneity.

Exercise 23: How Energized Is Your Workplace?

Being compassionate doesn't mean being serious all the time. Reflect upon your workplace, and then answer the questions below:

What do I and my colleagues do to energize our workplace through fun, play and spontaneity?

_____

_____

_____

_____

How much fun is my workplace? Circle the appropriate number below:

1   2   3   4   5   6   7   8   9   10

no fun at all   always fun

What new ways can I think of for energizing my workplace?

_____

_____

_____

_____

In the exercise below, you will have an opportunity to identify whether your workplace is a group, a team or a community. You will see that work groups tend to be less focused and less cohesive than teams, while workplace communities enjoy the highest levels of caring, passion and authenticity. Ultimately, you will be invited to think about how to develop your workplace into a genuine community where truly great things can happen.

Exercise 24: Is My Workplace a Group, a Team or a Community?

Below is a continuum of characteristics for groups, teams and workplace communities. Starting at the BOTTOM of the page, read the characteristics in ascending order.

Identify your workplace's level in the continuum.

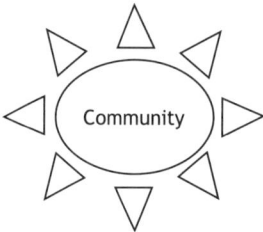

Community

12. Listen without judging; reflect without distorting; act as a reliable mirror
11. Reveal more of true Selves with each other (likes, dislikes, fears, aspirations)
10. Tell the truth
9. Have fun at work

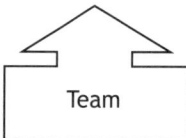

Team

8. Enjoy each other's company
7. Support each other
6. See the value of working together
5. Share a common goal

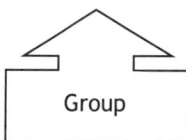

Group

4. Share information
3. Work independently of each other
2. Self-absorbed
1. Lack of common purpose

Next, generate at least three actions that you could take to move your workplace up the continuum toward genuine community. If you are already at the top of the continuum, what could you do to further strengthen your community?

Finally, invite your colleagues to do this exercise as well, and then discuss your ideas together.

• • •

In this chapter, you learned how to transform your workplace into a meaningful, mutually supportive community where great things can truly be accomplished. You also gained insights into how to see others as more than two-dimensional personifications of their work roles, and to see them instead as complete human beings. Lastly, you have seen that compassion in the workplace does not need to be serious all the time. Genuine workplace communities are fun places to work.

In Part Three of this book, "Your Relationship with the Higher Values," you will see that communities share and celebrate their Higher Values. They do not relegate these to the domain of the personal and private. Their values are revealed and treasured; they are incorporated into the fabric of everyday work life. The community, as a result, becomes richer and stronger.

It is not because each member of the community has the same set of beliefs or spiritual practices that the community is made stronger. Rather, it is the realization that the Higher Values are so universal that the community is able to learn and grow from the broad diversity of philosophical and spiritual expression of its members. This expression is incorporated into the functioning of the community, thereby enriching, strengthening and enlivening it and each of its members.

Love is what's in the room with you at Christmas
if you stop opening presents and listen.

Bobby, age 5

Part Three

Your Relationship with the Higher Values

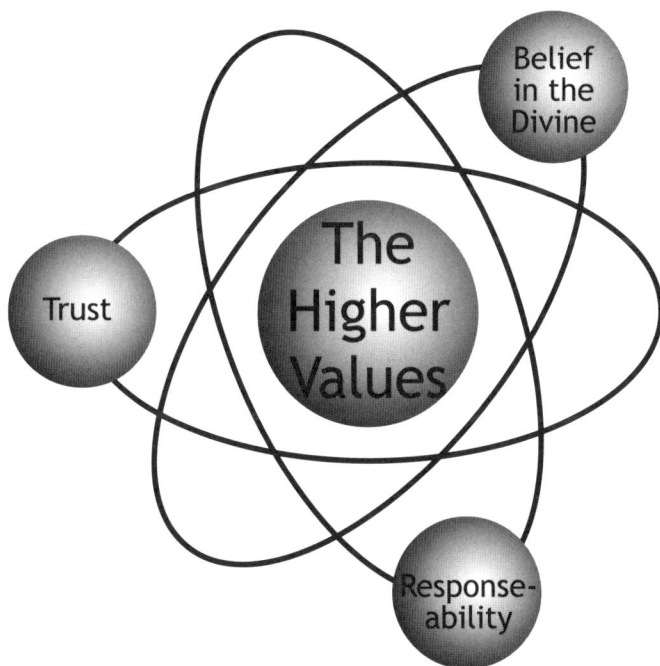

The secret to activating meaning and motivation in your work life is the development of three key relationships. In Part One, you explored the first relationship, your relationship with Self; in Part Two, you focused on your relationship with Others; and now in Part Three, you will examine the third and final relationship for bringing your work to life, your relationship with the Higher Values.

The Higher Values help you especially in situations where you are unclear about what to do or you simply need to muster your inner strength. The Higher Values also help you when there is a conflict between your beliefs and the beliefs of others. They provide you with a connection to the global community. They give you perspective. They enable you to take your nose off your particular window to the world so you realize that you've been looking through a lens—a lens that is fabricated from your own personal experiences and beliefs.

The Higher Values connect you to the web of consciousness that unites the world's diversity. In this way, the Higher Values constitute a wireless, spiritual universe. Just as technology allows you to *reach out and touch somebody*, the Higher Values allow you to reach out and touch *everybody*.

Furthermore, and importantly, the Higher Values provide you with a pathway to the Divine, that universal intelligence that is both within you and beyond you at the same time. Imagine that you are a drop of seawater. All of the elements of the ocean are within you, and yet you are not the ocean. The ocean is vast, powerful and unfathomable. So you, too, are limited in your ability to understand and know the Divine. It is like *seeing through a glass darkly*. Still, through your connection with the Higher Values, you can experience the Divine directly, and Part Three of the book will show you how.

You will begin by considering which Higher Values are most important to you at this time, and how best to make your relationship with them more present in your work life. You will then have an opportunity to explore your experience of the Divine. Finally, you will learn how to apply the Higher Values of Trust and Response-ability to your work life.

So where do the Higher Values come from and what are they, exactly?

If you were to study all of the world's greatest cultures, philosophies and spiritual traditions, you would discover that their values are all very similar, if not identical. While the practices vary, the values are the same. These values are so benevolent and so universal that they are referred to as the Higher Values, and they include such values as:

Belief in a Divine Intelligence
Love
Tolerance
Peace
Faith
Charity
Trust
Empathy
Service
Honesty
Integrity
Respect
Responsibility
Contribution

Exercise 25: My Higher Values

If you were to choose three Higher Values that are important to you right now, which three would you choose? What actions could you take to make each Higher Value more present in your work life? What contribution would each Higher Value make?

	Higher Value	**Actions**	**Contribution**
1.	_____	_____	_____
		_____	_____
		_____	_____
		_____	_____
		_____	_____
		_____	_____
2.	_____	_____	_____
		_____	_____
		_____	_____
		_____	_____
		_____	_____
		_____	_____
3.	_____	_____	_____
		_____	_____
		_____	_____
		_____	_____
		_____	_____
		_____	_____

Part Three of the book presents and expands upon three Higher Values in particular: belief in the divine, trust and response-ability. Although they are not more important than the ones you might wish to emphasize in your own work and life right now, the exploration of these particular Higher Values will not only enrich your work and personal life, but will also serve as a model to guide you in developing your relationship with the Higher Values of your own choosing.

Belief in the Divine

"Do you believe in God?"

Daniel was surprised by the question his colleague seemed to pose as a simple way of making conversation. They were walking along a narrow sidewalk in front of the Technical Training College in Zaria, Nigeria. The day was sweltering. They were at the beginning of a six-week project where they would be teaching and working closely together, so Daniel wasn't sure how to respond.

In the span of a mere two or three seconds, which felt more like 20 or 30 minutes, Daniel considered his options. If he were to answer "yes," then perhaps Sam would let it go at that. But what if Sam wanted to pursue it further and get into issues about the kind of God that Daniel believed in or the religion that he practiced? Truly, the unease that Daniel was experiencing was due more to the anticipated and inevitable religion debate than considering whether or not he believed in God.

Memories flashed through Daniel's mind. He thought about being brought up Catholic in a family of four boys. He remembered the mandatory going to church on Sundays and how boring it was. Latin, yuck! He remembered his all-boys Catholic high school and how the priests carried leather straps up the long, loose sleeves of their robes. He remembered how they all got the strap for things like being late for school, going down the "Up" staircase, getting a drink of water between periods, chewing gum, or walking with their hands in their pockets. It seemed he had earned more sins in his high school days than a lifetime of Confessions could possibly expunge. So, when he remembered his early experiences of religion, he remembered a childhood that oscillated between guilt and fear.

To counterbalance these recollections of his own religion, Daniel tried to think of his experiences with other religions. He didn't want to give Sam a distorted answer to his question. In the neighborhood where Daniel was brought up, on the outskirts of Toronto, he could remember people coming to the door every once in a while with various sorts of religious pamphlets. He remembered how they too had asked him if he believed in God, and how dissatisfied they seemed to be with the kind of God he believed in. They wanted very badly to change his way of thinking about God.

On the other hand, he could also remember how pleasant his mother was to these folks. She had a very nice way of talking to strangers about religion. However, he could also remember her hiding behind the couch on all fours one afternoon when she saw them coming up the driveway. She even sent him to the door to say she wasn't home. He tried to be as convincing as possible, although from the doorway, as he turned to go back to the living room, he could clearly see the tip of his mother's behind poking out from behind the couch. He thought it best never to mention this to her. It seems that even the anticipation of talking about religion can have a strange effect on the nicest of people.

Daniel's memory then shot back to when as a young teenaged boy in Montreal, he and his friend Pierre were debating how to best go about changing some of the behaviors of one of their friends. They wanted to change how their friend walked, how he talked, even how he chewed his food. Unbeknownst to them, however, Pierre's father had caught most of their conversation. Pierre's father was quite a sight. He only stood about five feet tall but was stocky and strong like a fireplug. He had tattoos on his forearms from his Navy days. Daniel had seen him take a casserole out of a 350-degree oven with his bare hands. He was a foreman in a heavy equipment factory. Nobody pushed him around. Or so Daniel imagined.

Anyway, Pierre's father interrupted their conversation. What he said was stated matter-of-factly and to the point. Daniel wasn't sure why he would remember such an event so many years later. Pierre's father had simply said, "You don't try to change people; you try to live with them."

What Pierre's father had expressed was a Higher Value—live and let live—and as such, it was an essential life lesson. If you contravene such a value, it always comes back to bite you. Perhaps that's why it stuck with him all these years.

If it is true that just before you die, your entire life flashes before your eyes in an instant, then Sam's question must have been a near-death experience for Daniel. But now at least he had his answer.

"Yes, Sam," Daniel replied calmly, "I do believe in God, but I don't believe in religion."

The effect of Daniel's answer on Sam would have been unmistakable even to a passerby, if one had been around. Sam gasped and was momentarily held speechless.

At that moment, it was not possible for Daniel to fully appreciate how astonishing it was to hold Sam speechless. After all, he only vaguely knew Sam. They rarely worked together and they didn't know each other outside of work either. So there was no way that Daniel could have known that Sam's father was a minister or that Sam himself had a doctoral degree in theology and was a lay minister in his church.

They took a few more steps in deafening silence until Sam noticed a long column of army ants marching in file along the sidewalk beside them. He reached into his pocket for a piece of chalk.

"Have you noticed this column of ants?" asked Sam in obvious excitement about what he was going to do next.

Daniel answered, "No, I hadn't noticed them. Interesting though, isn't it?"

"Indeed," continued Sam. "Watch what happens when I draw a line of chalk in front of the column."

With that, Sam drew his line and the ants immediately veered around it. Ants won't cross a chalk line.

"You see," said Sam, "religion is like that. It only guides us along our path. It provides us with the values that keep us on track, and ultimately makes us good people."

Daniel thought that Sam's lesson made a lot of sense. Wasn't that what Pierre's father had taught him so many years earlier? How to be a good person?

However, a question still nagged at Daniel, and so he blurted it out: "But Sam, who holds the chalk and who decides where the line is drawn?"

Sam smiled. It's not that Sam was stuck for words this time. He just decided to let it go. Sam knew from Daniel's responses that his experience was different from his own. What Sam had found in his church, Daniel had found amongst his family and friends, outside of formal religion.

It really wasn't important to either of them to pursue a debate. They both knew that what really mattered was how to get along; how to make your way peacefully in the world; how to make space for yourself as you also make space for others.

"I'm looking forward to working with you, Daniel," said Sam as he put one hand on his colleague's shoulder. "I'm looking forward to working with you, too," replied Daniel.

"Then how about coming to church with me on Sunday?" teased Sam. With that they both laughed and opened the door to the college.

Being religious and being spiritual can be two different things. Some people discover the Higher Values through their religious roots; some discover them outside of formal religion. It's no matter. What matters, as Daniel and Sam both acknowledged, is knowing how to get along; how to make your way peacefully in the world; and how to make space for yourself as you also make space for others.

Exercise 26: My Religious and Spiritual Roots

How would I describe my religious roots?

_____

_____

_____

_____

What impact does my religion have on the way I work and live?

_____

_____

_____

_____

Do I consider myself to be a "spiritual" person? What does this mean to me?

_____

_____

_____

_____

What impact does my spirituality have on the way I work and live?

_____

_____

_____

_____

What does it mean to bring your belief in the Divine to work with you? For one, it means always feeling loved unconditionally and always feeling forgiven absolutely. This, in turn, allows you to do your best and to offer all of your successes as well as all of your failures to the Divine. In this way, you know you cannot fail; you can only learn. Everything serves your growth. The workplace, and indeed life itself, become a classroom without walls. You engage in a process of lifelong learning as the workplace becomes energized through empowerment, encouragement and excellence.

Unfortunately, many people's experience of work is not nearly so positive. For example, have you ever had *just one of those days*? You know—a day when everything seemed to go wrong? Perhaps you had a fender-bender on the way to work, arrived late, went to the first meeting of the day unprepared; your boss yelled at you; you spilled your coffee, lost your patience and felt upset all day long? How then does the presence of the Divine in the workplace help you?

One way to access Divine help under these circumstances is to simply take the time to count your learnings. It's not exactly the same as counting your blessings, but in this instance it can amount to pretty much the same thing. What greater blessing than to be given the ability to learn from your most challenging work and life experiences!

Ultimately, counting your learnings can help refocus your attention and energy away from the unproductive and unhappy circumstances in your life, to the people, events and ideas that are far more productive and positive for you. Here is a simple yet effective way of going about counting your learnings, especially in trying circumstances.

Exercise 27: Count My Learnings

Think of a situation in your work life that is challenging to deal with right now. From the questions below, choose those that would be the most useful in helping you focus on the positive and productive so you can deal with your situation. Feel free to add to the list.

- What part of this situation is the most challenging for me?
- What part of this situation is the most comfortable for me?
- What can I learn from this?
- How could I handle this differently in the future?
- Who might be able to help me with this?
- What kind of help do I need?
- What can I do now?

- Which of my qualities will be most helpful to me now?
- How will my life be better once this situation is settled?
- If this situation were a blessing in disguise, what would the blessing be?
- What would be the most negative outcome that could result from this situation? How likely is this?
- What would be the most positive outcome that could result from this situation? How likely is this?
- What can I do to keep a positive outlook?

My Own Questions:

- _____
- _____
- _____
- _____

Of course, you don't need to believe in the Divine in order to reap the benefits of asking yourself these kinds of questions. In fact, if you remember to reflect upon them when you are facing a challenging situation, you will greatly enhance your ability to deal with it. You will utterly transform your attitude, feelings and behavior. You will become more empowered, positive, creative and confident. Ironically, you will become more divine.

Teresa is feeling anxious. She joined a medium-sized consulting firm 10 years ago, and is now a senior partner. She and a colleague are talking about a new contract. It requires designing, organizing and facilitating a series of mini-conferences right across North America, including Mexico. The president has asked Teresa to be one of the keynote speakers since the results of the Effectiveness Audit that she implemented will form the basis of discussion at each of the conferences.

"What a blast!" exclaims Leila. "This is an incredible opportunity."

"What do you mean?" Teresa replies. "For me, this is a death sentence!"

Leila can't believe her ears. "You've got to be kidding. This will be great fun. Can you imagine 500 people gathered in a hall somewhere, just to hear you! Wow!"

"Look, you don't seem to realize I'm scared to death!"

"But you do this all the time. You're good at it."

"But I'm always scared," Teresa confides. "I think I'm a little high-strung. By the way, how do you manage to keep so calm?"

"What do you mean?" asks Leila sheepishly.

"You know," says Teresa. "You're as cool as the proverbial cucumber!"

"Do you really want to know?" checks Leila with just a hint of suspicion in her voice.

"Yes, I do. I really want to know," Teresa insists.

"Well, I meditate." Leila states somewhat tentatively.

"What in the world does that mean!" Teresa asks with a little bit of exasperation in her voice.

"I know it's a little different, but I find it very relaxing. I would even say that it has helped build my confidence."

"Are you religious or something?" questions Teresa.

"In a way, perhaps. I do practice Hinduism. But you don't need to be religious to meditate. You don't even have to believe in God, if you don't want to. It's just a good practice for relaxation."

"I see," Teresa ponders. "Maybe I should give it a try."

"Perhaps you should. Apart from drugs, it's the best method I know for becoming calmer in everyday life!"

"What!" exclaims Teresa.

"Just kidding," reassures Leila. "I'll show you how to meditate if you want, but don't be surprised if you feel the hand of God on your shoulder while you're doing it."

"Heavy!" quips Teresa.

"No, not really. Her hand is actually quite light and reassuring!" teases Leila.

Have you ever meditated? You just sit. Do nothing. Don't even think. You just hold the emptiness of the silence inside you. When you experience the silence, you also experience the Divine. The Divine is the fullness that you feel in the emptiness of the silence. It is a feeling of calm and completeness. You can experience this and know it for yourself, if you want to.

Of course, the benefits of meditation are very well known. There are two primary benefits. First, you can relax immediately when you meditate. Like watching the leaves falling from the trees in autumn, you will feel the stress leaving your body. Within just three minutes, you can reduce the number of times your heart beats by about 10 beats per minute. That's a lot less wear and tear on your heart and on your entire system. It's rejuvenating and relaxing.

Secondly, there is a distinct, cumulative benefit to meditating regularly. You will become more and more calm in your work and in your life generally. You will feel relaxed, centered and clear-headed no matter what the circumstances. This is important because it is one thing to be relaxed while you're meditating in the quiet of your own room, but it's quite another to be calm and in control while you're in an emotional meeting or stuck in traffic.

Even if you could only spare 60 seconds out of every 24 hours for meditating, you would experience enormous benefits.

> *You do not need to leave your room.*
> *Remain sitting at your table and listen.*
> *Do not even listen; simply wait.*
> *Do not even wait. Be quiet, still and solitary.*
> *The world will freely offer itself to you to be unmasked.*
> *It has no choice. It will roll in ecstasy at your feet.*
> Franz Kafka

Exercise 28: Meditation

1. Sit quietly in a comfortable position.

2. Close your eyes.

3. Deeply relax all your muscles, beginning at your feet and progressing up to your face.

4. Breathe comfortably—preferably through your nose, but be comfortable in your breathing. Focus on the breath. Allow the silence to

envelop you. If thoughts enter your mind, do not pursue them. Quietly observe and allow them to leave of their own accord.

5. Continue like this for 10 to 15 minutes. When you finish, transition slowly to your next activity.

• • •

In meditation, there is nothing to do. This is why many people find it challenging. Meditation is about being, not doing. If thoughts are like the boxcars on a moving train, meditation occurs in the spaces between the cars.

Keep a relaxed focus, without judgment. Allow your thoughts to occur. Observe them come in and move out like the waves on a beach. No need to push them out. They will leave on their own. No need to think these thoughts, either. Just observe without judgment. Meditation is a practice: a path, not a destination.

It's a hot August morning and Ross finds himself watching a curious little friend on the riverbank as he sits alone in his canoe. The sweet smell of juniper is in the air as a crowd of bulrushes sways gently to and fro in the soft summer breeze. Faint shadows criss-cross the large space between the bulrushes and the orchard, and he knows this is worrying his little friend. As he looks up he sees several hawks gliding like kites across the sun. The mouse trembles as he contemplates crossing the space into the orchard.

This reminds Ross of his own situation. He has been a self-employed consultant for eight years, and each year has been a test of faith. His last contract was in May; it's nearly September and he still doesn't have many prospects of work. His line of credit is slowly being whittled away. He's married with two children. His wife is self-employed too, and her work prospects don't look any better than his. Mortgage payments and other expenses continue to pile up.

He recalls how he felt about all of this yesterday morning. In fact, he was trembling just like his little friend, the mouse. His heart was pounding as he contemplated how he would cross the space between his increasing debt on the one side and some sense of financial security on the other. It was when he was feeling the most frightened that he decided to pray.

He began simply by focusing his awareness on his breath, reminding himself that he was still alive, calming himself, and clearing his mind as best he could. He then disclosed how frightened he was and asked to be forgiven for this because he knew that he'd always been taken care of in the past. He ended by declaring that although he still felt afraid, he chose to have faith, and he asked for help in doing so.

He opened his eyes and started downstairs when the miracle happened. The phone rang. It was someone whom Ross hadn't spoken with in over two years. She worked for one of his client organizations and was calling to ask if he would do a project for her. Moreover, she urged him to send in his invoice immediately because she had to clear the money out of her budget before the end of the month. In the time it took to answer the phone, his financial security was regained and his faith restored.

Today, Ross is enjoying the end of a long, hot summer. As he noses his canoe into the current, he glances back at the trembling mouse. Ross silently prays that his little friend might cross safely through the space between the bulrushes and the orchard. He wishes him Godspeed on his journey, for today he realizes they are both travellers sharing the same path.

Are you familiar with the expression, "Be careful what you ask for; you just might get it!" Well, this is true for prayer. Be careful what you ask for, but do ask. *Ask and you shall receive.* You might not get what you want, but you will always get what you need. The Divine has broad shoulders, big enough to take on your worries, the next person's worries, and more. So pray for what you need.

Exercise 29: The Power of Prayer

Describe a time when your prayers were answered.

_____

_____

_____

_____

Prayers can be used to express your needs, to express your gratitude, or to help others:

What do you really need, right now?

_____

_____

_____

_____

What are you grateful for in your work and in your life?

_____

_____

_____

_____

Who needs your prayers right now? What do they need?

_____

_____

_____

_____

Some people have a favorite prayer. What is yours?

_____

_____

_____

_____

Belief in the Divine is the most basic of all the Higher Values. It is the platform upon which all the other Higher Values stand. The Divine is the universal and loving intelligence that is both within you and beyond you at the same time.

Nonetheless, you can experience the Divine directly by counting your learnings, practicing meditation and unleashing the power of prayer. When you count your learnings, you become positive and empowered. You face workplace challenges with confidence and perseverance. When you practice meditation, you become relaxed and resourceful, even in the face of adversity. And when you unleash the power of prayer, you tap into a force of unimaginable strength. You see opportunities instead of obstacles, possibilities in the place of problems.

In the next chapter, you will examine the Higher Value of trust. You will see that being able to trust in the face of great change and uncertainty is very closely connected to the belief in the Divine. On balance, trust is easier when you believe that the situation in which you find yourself has been divinely created. Trust allows you to relax and accept the reality of what is present before taking action. This enables the action to be better thought out and, ultimately, more effective. Just as Ross chose to have faith even though he was afraid, trust is also a choice. When you choose to trust, you allow yourself to move forward, knowing that in any situation you can only hold yourself responsible for doing your best. The rest is beyond your control anyway. So the next chapter will show you how to trust—even when you don't!

Trust

How do you trust when you don't trust? When life and work become challenging, it is easy to forget that trust is a choice. This chapter will help you to choose to trust even in the most trying situations. It focuses on nurturing that profound and fundamental trust that can allow you to meet your life and work demands with energy, confidence and optimism.

This kind of trust keeps hope alive. It means believing that everything will turn out for the best; that you will be taken care of, and that every challenge is accompanied by an opportunity. Ultimately, this kind of trust is a leap of faith.

This chapter will show you how to nurture trust and to develop a sense of the positive, a sense of faith. Nowhere is this more needed than in the face of change and uncertainty. In fact, even the changes that you yourself strive to bring about are often accompanied by high levels of anxiety, fear and doubt. This chapter will show you how to develop the trust you need to reduce the potency of these debilitating feelings so you can apply the best of you to what you do.

> For the past 18 months, Steve and Suzanne have been studying the feasibility of opening a coffee shop. As neither one of them has had previous retail experience, they have taken a very methodical and detailed approach to assessing their mutual business venture. Their working relationship has been very positive and pleasant. Both of them are typically good-natured.
>
> Unexpectedly, an ideal location for their prospective coffee shop has come up. But, in order to secure it, they need to move fast because

other people are looking at it, too. If they decide to take it, they need to make a significant financial commitment. This is worrisome for them both. At least in the research stage, all they committed was their own personal energy. Now it's time to put in money. What's more, this is just the beginning. If they go ahead, money will need to be spent on refurbishing, supplies, incorporation, staff, and so on.

For the first time, friction and irritability are starting to creep into their relationship, and each of them is beginning to conjure up negative fantasies about working with the other. Will Steve want to take control of the business? Will he do his fair share of set-up and clean-up? Will Suzanne do more socializing with the customers than actual working? Will she want to have her way in terms of décor? Will this relationship become a nightmare? Both their heads seem to be filled with questions and worries.

What to do? Of course, they need to talk. But what kind of conversation is this going to be if they bring such negativity into their interaction? It's likely to be hysterical at best. Therefore, before they talk, they each need to take a deep breath; call a time out; take a walk in silence; meditate; do whatever it takes to rediscover their trust and faith in each other and in the natural process of life.

Once trust is chosen, life will begin to support them in whatever they need. It is as if trust were a doorway; once they cross the threshold, they will begin to receive the support they need to deal with the challenges of the situation in which they find themselves.

Steve and Suzanne will begin to realize that what they are going through and how they are feeling are not unique. They are not alone. Others have formed partnerships and opened businesses, too. Many of them have not only survived but have thrived in the process.

They will begin to think about the bigger picture. The preparations for their grand opening will soon be a memory. It's just the beginning of their working relationship. They have a long way to *grow*.

They will begin to remind themselves of the feelings and personal qualities that brought them together in the first place. They will rediscover the respect they have for each other. They will be reassured that whatever the obstacles they encounter along their path, they can communicate, support each other and persevere.

This is trust in action. The person who chooses to trust is calm, positive, action-oriented and confident.

> Gerald has worked for Pronto Courier Service for the past 11 years. Due to the latest downswing in the economy, huge layoffs at many local companies and the influx of new competition, Pronto's business has decreased dramatically. So today, Gerald is one of two employees who were handed their pink slips.
>
> He understands the reasons for his being laid off. They're based on logical explanations about the local economy and his seniority. But this doesn't help him feel any better. In fact, in some ways he feels worse because he is angry but has no target for his anger. He can't blame his boss. His boss made the only decision he could, based on business levels and head count. He can't blame his union. The company is following the rules laid down by the Collective Agreement. He could try to blame the economy, but that's a little vague as a target. The government? What could they do? The competition? Who can blame them for trying to make a living? So he's stuck with his feelings of anger, frustration and anxiety.
>
> Tonight he will go home to his wife and break the news to her. Fortunately, her job with the government is probably secure. But, like most

families, they have come to rely on two wages. They will undoubtedly have questions and concerns about a whole range of things, like Gerald's severance package, mortgage and other payments, university tuition for their two children, benefits and insurance coverage, and on the list goes.

Does Gerald trust that everything happens for his highest possible good? Does he really think that he and his family will be okay? Is he willing to look upon his layoff as an opportunity? Is he ready to trust in the natural process of life? Probably not.

Many years ago, Dr. Murray Banks, a renowned psychiatrist, teased the audience during a speech by asking a rhetorical question: "What is the difference between a neurotic and a psychotic? Well, a neurotic is the person who builds sand castles in the air, while a psychotic is the person who moves in. And the therapist is the one who comes by once a month to collect the rent!"

You see, feelings of anger, frustration and anxiety are perfectly normal and healthy—for a while. They are the stone and mortar that make up our sand castles. And our sand castles are okay to visit, but not to live in. Know when you're moving in and know when to move out. The exit door is trust, and once you open it to leave, you begin to see how life supports you.

However, just as with Steve and Suzanne, it takes a little time. So remember to be gentle with yourself. Take a deep breath. Remind yourself that you're still alive. Call a time out; take a walk in silence; meditate; give yourself permission to do whatever you need in order to come back to your trust and faith in yourself and in the people around you. Give yourself a chance to come back to your trust and faith in the natural process of life.

Gerald's experience is not unique. Others have gotten laid off too. In fact, many of them have made very successful transitions. He can too. He needs to look at the bigger picture. At some point, losing his job will only be a memory. He's at the beginning of the rest of his career.

He needs to remind himself of the kinds of people who are supporting him, like his wife, children, other family members, friends and colleagues. Undoubtedly, there have been times before when he, with the help of others, has overcome other obstacles.

If Gerald can learn to trust in this way, he will then be able to take the action he needs to get through this. Gradually, he can become a person who is calm, positive, action-oriented and confident. He might even find one day that he's a better person for having been laid off than if this had never happened to him.

How many people have gone through very trying circumstances, only to find they were really a blessing in disguise! They are grateful for the learning they have gained as a result of it. The strongest steel has gone through the hottest fire.

In the following exercise, you will have an opportunity to reflect upon a trying situation that you have come through. Take a moment now to think of such a situation—in your personal life or your work life. What was the role that trust played in your situation? What impact did it have? Your answers to the exercise provide the keys that you need to handle trying situations successfully.

Exercise 30: Nurturing Trust

Describe a situation in which you found it difficult to trust.

_____

_____

_____

_____

At what point did you decide to trust? If you didn't decide to trust, what motivated your actions in dealing with the situation?

_____
_____
_____
_____

What were the consequences of not trusting?

_____
_____
_____
_____

What were the consequences of trusting?

_____
_____
_____
_____

When you're facing difficult situations, like change and uncertainty, what can you do to help yourself keep trust alive?

_____
_____
_____
_____

Fear, anger and frustration are powerful motivators for dealing with change and uncertainty. Trust is not the only source of motivation. But what are the consequences of being motivated by feelings such as anger versus being motivated by feelings such as trust? Negative emotions create a lot of wear and tear on the individual who holds them. It's not that these negative emotions are not strong enough to energize you to take action. It's rather that they are too strong and unpredictable; they often lead to stress, depression and even panic.

In this way, negative emotions prevent you from performing at your best. This is why trust is so important. Trusting that everything will turn out for the best engenders feelings of hope, optimism and confidence. These, in turn, allow you to take purposeful action in a spirit of empowerment, discovery and learning. Ultimately, trust is a very healthy and useful force in your work and in your life. It can unlock the full power of your potential.

In the next chapter, you will see how once trust is in place, action naturally follows. Once you trust, you empower yourself to act. You begin to exercise your ability to respond to the circumstances that have been presented to you. The next chapter will focus on how to enhance this ability to respond, thereby strengthening your "response-ability."

Response-ability

Taking responsibility is the first step in the process of change. It is a step that creates self-empowerment. The opposite of taking responsibility is placing blame. Blaming is a step that creates self-disempowerment. You give your power away to whomever or whatever you blame. Blaming depletes your ability to respond. Taking responsibility increases your ability to respond— your response-ability.

In this way, response-ability is the mental muscle you flex in order to bring about change in yourself, in others and in the larger community. Response-ability provides the power through which all your ideas are materialized. Unless you exercise your response-ability, your ideas will remain relegated to the realm of the theoretical, thereby failing the test of the practical. As long as your ideas are merely theories, they will never be put into practice.

The chart below illustrates the connection between language and your level of response-ability. Notice the differences between the kinds of words in the column on the left and those in the column on the right. The way you talk to yourself and to others is a key indicator of whether you orient yourself toward being irresponsible or being response-able in any given situation. The language is much more positive, empowering and action-oriented in the "Response-able" column, talking to yourself in this way enhances your ability to respond.

Irresponsible	**Response-able**
I'm not responsible.	I am response-able.
Why did this have to happen?	What can I learn?
Why me, Lord?	What can I do, now?
I'll try.	I'll do it.
I hate to bother you, but if you have a chance, I'd really appreciate it if…	I need your help.

For example, suppose unexpectedly on your way home from work, you get a flat tire. You're tired. It's raining. You're late for dinner. What do you say to yourself after you pull onto the side of the road? Perhaps in utter exasperation you complain, *why did this have to happen to me?* Maybe you swear a little, too!

Of course, none of this helps very much. After all, you've still got the flat tire. At best, you might let off some steam. But now what? Well, now it's time for action and you can become either your own worst enemy or your own best friend. You can either make the situation even more difficult for yourself or you can make it easier to deal with.

If your enemy came by just as you had pulled onto the side of the road, what would he or she say to you? If your best friend happened to come by just as you had pulled onto the side of the road, what would he or she say to you? Compare the two lists, below.

Worst Enemy	Best Friend
Hi, Loser! Ever wonder why bad things always happen to you?	Hi, my friend. I see it's your turn to get the flat tire. I got a flat tire a couple of years ago not too far from here.
Too bad it's raining; you're going to get soaked. You'll be cold, wet and miserable.	Ever see Cary Grant in *Singing in the Rain?* Remember, there are worse things than getting wet. Pretend you're a kid—enjoy it!
The jack probably won't work. Even if it does, you've never used one before.	Let's check the car manual first. This is probably very straightforward.
You'll never get that tire changed.	The tire should be easy to change. If not, you've got a cell phone. Call for help.
You're probably going to get killed doing this!	Remember to take some basic safety precautions and everything will be all right.

When you think about it, if you talked to others the way you talk to yourself, you might not have many friends. It's important to treat yourself the way your best friend would treat you. It's more positive and empowering that way. It gives you the best chance of doing your best.

Response-ability Matrix

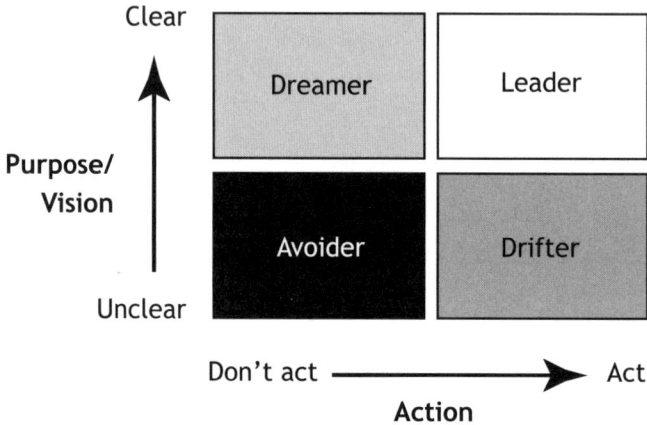

In the Response-ability Matrix, you will notice that response-ability consists of two dimensions: purpose/vision and action. The juxtaposition of these two dimensions creates four possible kinds of response-ability.

Avoider

This describes a person who is unclear about their purpose and vision, and who does not take action. They allow work and life to take place around them. They do not contribute in any meaningful way. They are like the handle on the pot—they are there, but they're not "in it." In order to increase their response-ability, they need to answer the questions "Who am I and what do I want?" Once this is done, they can then consider what would be the easiest step they could take that would move them in the direction of their purpose/vision.

Drifter

Unlike the Avoider, the Drifter does indeed take action. However, it is not purposeful. They lack a sense of purpose and vision. They might latch onto a project here and there, or change jobs, roles and organizations from time to time, but their actions are haphazard. They contribute sporadically. They don't stick. They're like sagebrush rolling in the wind. In order to increase their response-ability, they also need to work on their answers to the questions "Who am I and what do I want?"

Dreamer

The Dreamer is like the Avoider in that they don't take action. However, they have a fairly clear sense of purpose and vision—they're simply not following through. This might be due to self-doubt, or perhaps a lack of commitment. In order to increase their response-ability, they need to reaffirm their belief in the Higher Values, such as trust, then exercise their mental muscles and just do it!

Leader

The Leader is a person who has a clear sense of purpose and vision. They make a reliable contribution to themselves and others. They have a deep sense of work and life satisfaction and serve as a valuable role model. The potential challenges with this role most likely involve work–life balance. This balance is always dynamic and requires constant vigilance.

Exercise 31:   My Level of Response-ability

Think of a challenging situation in your work and another in your personal life. Relative to these situations, in which quadrant of the Response-Ability Matrix would you place yourself, right now? What are the consequences of being in this quadrant? How might you enhance your level of response-ability?

Quadrant	**Consequences**	**Enhancement Strategies**

Work

_____   _____   _____

_____   _____   _____

_____   _____   _____

_____   _____   _____

_____   _____   _____

_____   _____   _____

Personal Life

_____   _____   _____

_____   _____   _____

_____   _____   _____

_____   _____   _____

_____   _____   _____

_____   _____   _____

In the following excerpt from the fable *Children of the Root*, * Rootkin Elder is teaching Willy about the three kinds of Rootkins who live in the underground.

On one of Willy's visits to the old cavern, Rootkin Elder told him, "There are three kinds of Rootkins: dreamers, drifters and leaders. The dreamers possess great vision and a clear sense of purpose but, alas, they do not take action. Their path is the path of broken dreams. The drifters are in constant motion but do not possess vision. Their path is one of aimless pursuit. Finally, the leaders not only possess great vision but they also act with purpose. Theirs is the path of great things. You must decide which kind of Rootkin you want to be."

Willy thought about what Rootkin Elder had said.

"It's too bad that there are so many dreamers and drifters," he replied finally.

"No, it isn't," answered Rootkin Elder, shaking her head. "It is natural that there are so many dreamers and drifters in the underground. They are perfect exactly the way they are. If they could do better, they'd be doing so right now. It is also natural that there are leaders to show them the way. They, too, are perfect exactly the way they are. You see, we are all on a path, doing the best we can. We are all filled with the invisible energy of the universe. We are all needed to nourish the life creatures. We are all children of the root."

Some people spend their entire lives and careers in one particular quadrant of the Response-Ability Matrix; other people spend some time in all four, depending on a multitude of factors. However, it is important to remember that there is no benefit in judging others or yourself. We are all doing the best we

---

*To receive a free copy of the book *Children of the Root* (a retail value of $10.00) by Bill Mills, please send $4.00 to cover postage and handling to InnerFormation Inc., 5511 Wicklow Drive, Manotick, ON, Canada K4M 1C4.

can. Keep in mind, though, that when you're ready, you can enhance your ability to respond to life and work situations by developing your sense of purpose and vision, and by simply making the decision to act. Vision and action are the heart and soul of leadership, and everyone has the potential to be a leader.

Response-ability, like trust, is a choice. You need to choose to be response-able. It is the mental muscle you flex in order to bring about change in yourself, others and the larger community.

Response-ability is the force that empowers you, moves you through the process of desicion making and into action. It helps you realize that for change to happen, you must act. Ultimately, it helps you realize that the change you desire is already within your grasp.

Bring Your Work to Life:
Applying the Best of You to What You Do!

Work is the sandbox of life. It's where grown-ups go to play. And since you spend at least half of your waking moments at work, it's important that you derive as much meaning as possible from this experience. Meaning, in turn, is a very powerful motivator, and leads to both personal and organizational success.

The focus of *Bring Your Work to Life: Applying the Best of You to What You Do!* is to provide you with some important insights into how you can bring your own work to life; and how you can derive more meaning and motivation from the workplace. It really has a lot to do with relationships.

Relationships are to life what the atom is to matter. They are the fundamental building blocks of existence. Relationships are not just important; they are all that matters. Therefore, the secret to activating meaning and motivation in your work life is the exploration and development of three key relationships:

- Your Relationship with Self—connecting with who you are and what you want;
- Your Relationship with Others—connecting with people as individuals and as teams;
- Your Relationship with the Higher Values—connecting with life's universal principles

Exercise 32: Bringing My Work to Life:
Applying the Best of Me to What I Do

What one idea, goal or action would most help me strengthen my relationship with my Self?

_____

_____

_____

_____

What one idea, goal or action would most help me strengthen my relationship with the important individuals and teams in my workplace?

_____

_____

_____

_____

What one idea, goal or action would most help me strengthen my relationship with the Divine and the other Higher Values that are most important to me?

_____

_____

_____

_____

If I took only one small step toward transforming my work life into a more meaningful and motivating experience, what would that step be?

_____

_____

_____

_____

Life is short—and at least half of it is spent at work. So seize the opportunity that this book offers. Instill more meaning and motivation into your work. Bring your work to life. Apply the best of you to what you do. Get up Monday morning saying to yourself, "Thank God it's Monday; I get to go to work again today!"

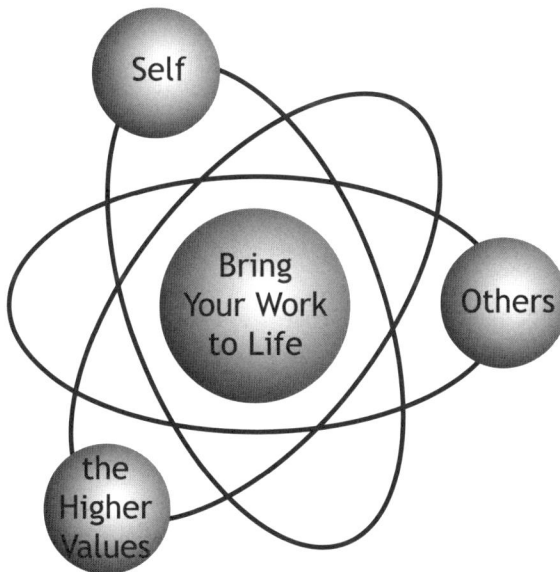

Index of Exercises in *Bring Your Work to Life*

Creative Bound Resources

a division of Creative Bound Inc.

Resources for personal growth and enhanced performance

www.creativebound.com

A speakers bureau with a unique offering! Our speakers are published experts in a variety of lifestyle areas, including stress control and life balance, motivation, leadership development and enhancement of personal and professional performance. They deliver their message in an upbeat, entertaining and accomplished fashion. Presentations are tailored to the needs and goals of each group for optimal impact.

William J. Mills, M.Ed.

An inspirational author and stimulating presenter, **Bill Mills** is committed to bringing more compassion, community and meaning to the workplace. Since 1987, he has been vice-president of InnerFormation Training and Consulting Incorporated (www.innerformation.ca), a consulting firm specializing in personal, leadership and team development. Bill has worked in both the public and private sectors, and has managed training and development projects across Canada and in the US, Mexico, Argentina, Italy and Nigeria.

Bill is a sought-after workshop facilitator and keynote speaker. For more information on his keynote presentations, seminars and team-building workshops, please contact Creative Bound Inc. at 1-800-287-8610 or visit our website at **www.creativebound.com**.

**To receive a free information package,
please contact Creative Bound Resources at 1-800-287-8610
or by e-mail at resources@creativebound.com**

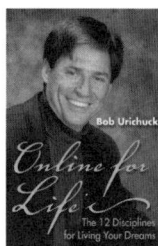

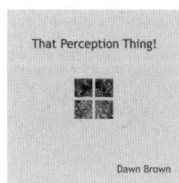